Greasepa... and Gore

The Hammer Monsters of

Roy ASHTON

To Trumpy

Bruce Sachs and Russell Wall

*Don't read this book with the lights out!
(oH! you want se able to.) Trump Trump Trump.
Love od
Best wishes*

Tomahawk Press

Sheffield, England

Designed by Steve Kirkham

Published by Tomahawk Press
PO Box 1236, Sheffield, South Yorkshire S11 7XU England
e-mail: press@tomahawk.globalnet.co.uk

ISBN 0 9531926 0 1

Printed and bound in Great Britain by The Design and Print Partnership, Avalon House, Beehive Lane, Chelmsford, Essex CM2 9TE England. Telephone 01245 269361 Fax 01245 269362

Acknowledgements...

The authors wish to thank all of those who have given their time, resources, and support to this project. The support and help we have received from the international network of Hammer fans has been overwhelming, and we thank them on behalf of Roy, to whom they have demonstrated their devotion. Our thanks also goes out to Hammer Films Ltd., for their encouraging support. We also wish to thank the many individuals who have given up hours of their time to be interviewed by us, and to tell them how much we enjoyed speaking with them. Their contributions have been invaluable. We wish to offer special thanks to a number of individuals who have sacrificed considerable time and energy into helping us, without whom this book would have been impossible: Harry Nadler and all the rest at the Fantastic Films Society, Dr. Wayne Kinsey, Christopher Lee, John Gold, Michael Harvey and Paul Goodman at The National Museum of Photography, Film and Televison, Jonathan Young, Steve Kirkham, Uwe Sommerlad, Dick Klemensen, Peter Leakey, Mrs. Elizabeth Ashton, David Aldous, Pat Sachs and Susan Wild.

All photograghs, drawings, and illustrations in this book are protected by copyright. The majority are owned by the Ashton estate. Tomahawk Press would like to thank Graham Skeggs at Hammer Films for his kind permission to reproduce photographs. Any specific enquiries about copyright ownership should be directed to the publishers. Films are referenced by release dates. Supplemental photography was provided by Bruce Sachs.

Forthcoming Titles from Tomahawk Press:

Somebody Mentioned Horror: A Posthumous Autobiography by Phil Leakey
By Russell Wall and Bruce Sachs

Behind the Scenes at Hammer: The Cast and Crew Speak for Themselves*
By Wayne Kinsey with B. Sachs and R. Wall

Patchwork: Diary of a Scream Queen
By Hazel Court

*Watch out for our companion video releases for this book and the
ones above – Coming Soon!*

* working title

Contents

Prologue by Peter Cushing

Prologue by Peter Cushing

"Little dabs of powder

Little drops of paint

makes ladies faces

Look like what they ain't"

That old saw could well be the motto of that unsung hero of the film world, the makeup artist.

Unless he is called upon to use his skills in creating some transfiguration (as did Jack Pierce for Boris Karloff as the "monster" in Universal's 1931 Frankenstein), his subtle contribution to the quality of a motion picture is regarded not!

On many occasions, it has been my pleasure and privilege to be looked after in this department by Roy Ashton, one of the very best in the business.

Always smiling, always attentive, this gentle gentleman soothed the nerves early in the morning, cleverly hiding the ravages of time, and keeping a discreet silence when he noticed I was muttering my lines for the day's work ahead.

Roy did a considerable amount of pencil sketches as guides for some of his creations, and how enterprising of Mr. Bruce Sachs and Mr. Russell Wall of Tomahawk Press to gather these together and have them published! As well as providing an interesting glimpse into this magic world of make-believe, it is also a fitting tribute to one who deserves his praises sung, as he is far too modest to do so himself.

PETER CUSHING

August 1991

7

FOREWORD
by Elizabeth Ashton

Being the wife of a make-up artist is not dull. There are times, of course, when he is away for long stretches, in various parts of the globe, and the preparations for such trips vary according to the venue.

The tropics mean getting out the bush shirts, the Northern climes mean warm sweaters and sheepskin hats. His passport must be in order, and all the make-up kit must be complete and ready for all emergencies - there are no cosmetic shops in the desert!

Above:
Elizabeth and Roy Ashton

When Roy was working on a "straight" film, with only beautiful women and handsome men to be glamourised, things were not too difficult, unless there were beards to clean and dress ready for the next day's shooting, and he would have a little more time to himself in the evenings. If there were night shots of course, this meant standing around in the street, or wherever the chosen site was for shooting, hour after hour. Usually on such occasions, there would be a caravan for the make-up department, parked somewhere nearby.

Some films create rather more work for the department, where there are men with wounds etc. as in *Dunkirk*. I remember Roy telling me how he had a disagreement with the director (Leslie Norman) one day on that film. John Mills was the leading actor, and was supposed to have been on the road for two weeks with his platoon, sheltering in hedges by day, and moving at night to avoid the enemy, as they made their way to the coast of France. The director said they were too dirty, and that John Mills was unrecognisable. Roy had to point out that a clean face was not likely to have much credence after the ordeal the platoon was supposed to have gone through! This location was in England, at Camber Sands on the south coast, and the film was one of the most gruelling that Roy ever worked on. Shooting began in the early morning, which meant getting out to the location from the hotel, with no breakfast, since the hotel staff had not yet come on duty, making-up the major and minor artists, and then putting bloody bandages and dirty grey greasepaint on dozens of "soldiers" ready for shooting to start at eight a.m. One morning Roy had been hard at work for two hours, on an empty stomach, and was ready for the canteen wagon when he was told to stand-by for shooting. He said he was off to get his breakfast, and walked off in no mood for any argument! Incidentally, he brought home some large bottles of imitation blood after that film, and some of it was on his clothes. I never could get it off, and it dried hard! When a friend saw some towels with the "blood" on, she thought we had had some dreadful accident!

In North Africa, working on *Sea of Sand* with Richard Attenborough, the unit stayed in Tetuan for part of the time, and had a hair-raising journey by taxi every morning to the location, around mountainous roads on the edges of precipices at a breakneck speed. Indeed, one car went over the edge during the time Roy was there. I don't think any of the film crew were in it at the time, but the driver was killed. The sand, as fine as flour, got into everything, and Roy's make-up boxes had to be vacuumed out when he came home. He told me some of the crew had stupidly removed their shirts in the heat, and had suffered very badly from sunburn. Roy was well aware of the folly of this, born and brought up in Australia as he was. He had a wide variety of hats, from denim to leather lined with sheepskin, and always took the appropriate headgear away with him, or else bought some suitable straw hat in a local shop or bazaar.

In the earlier years of our marriage, we were both earning a living as professional singers. Roy was a very fine tenor, and sang many performances of opera, being a Founder Member of Benjamin Britten's English Opera Group, as well as singing such roles as Faust, and Entr'Acte Operas by Pergolesi, Purcell, and many other composers. His earlier training in film make-up gave him a good living ultimately, when he found that singing brought in rather less money than we needed.

I remember on one occasion when Roy came home, instead of opening the door with his key, he rang the doorbell. When I answered it, there he stood, with a superb beard on. He really looked very distinguished, but I found the whiskery kiss was less than pleasant. His father always had a beard, and I wonder now whether he had tried it on to see if I liked the look of him with one!

In the early days, Roy used to work 7am to midnight, then 7am again the next day, weekends included. No overtime! At one time he had no day off for two years, and had very little sleep. This was just before the war. He became so ill that he was given a month's leave in July 1939. He bought a little car (which used more oil than petrol!), and went to Cornwall to surf. A month later the war came. What a life!

When Roy returned to the film industry, he was amazed at the improvement in conditions of employment, thanks to the involvement of the National Association of Television and Kine Employees.

When Roy first went to Bray Studios to help Phil Leakey on one of the Hammer Horrors, we were living in Surbiton. His work there was interesting, and when the company asked him to take over the department, after Phil left, he had ample opportunity to exercise his imagination and ingenuity.

Roy had a wonderful sense of the ridiculous, and revelled in the nonsense that he had to dream up for those horror pictures. When he made Oliver Reed up as the Werewolf, he tried many ways to get the best "animal" look, and spent hours drawing various possible masks, or part-masks, before his final choice. He had been to the Natural History Museum, in London, to look at wolves and other dogs, to find the right shape to fit on Oliver's head. When he needed to make the nostrils flare he put pieces of candle, minus the wick, into the nose. Oliver had to breathe through the empty wick-holes.

Roy came home with an amusing anecdote one day. The night before, there had been a party to celebrate the end of the film, which was *Paranoiac*, if my memory serves me correctly. The skeleton, which Roy had made with eyeballs filled with eggshells, and some pieces of cloth hanging from the arms etc., to represent a man who had been walled up for several years, had taken pride of place during the party. Afterwards, this horror had been taken up to the make-up room and flung into the old dentists' chair which was used for the actors to sit in while being made-up. The next morning, a cleaning lady went into the room, and the sight which met her eyes gave her such a shock that she ran screaming down the corridor!

Foreword

Sometimes Roy would have a sleepless night, trying to invent some wearable piece of equipment to look like whatever terrifying creature the writer had visualised. I used to wonder that he didn't have nightmares, but he himself used to say that all those strange films were really comic-cuts, and he didn't believe any harm would come to those who saw the films. Certainly, their continuing popularity would seem to bear this out, and indeed, when one sees some of the horror pictures of more recent production, with the inevitable sex scenes and perversion of all kinds, I think the Hammer Horrors were quite wholesome!

Roy Ashton was the kindest and gentlest of men, and in the forty-seven years we were married I was fortunate to have such a faithful husband, a much loved and respected man by all who knew him, and my best friend. I rejoice in his life, which brought so much pleasure to so very many people all over the world.

Elizabeth Ashton.

Introduction

> **If you are fascinated by the horrors on the cinema screen you are in distinguished company, for many celebrated artists and writers have pursued the grotesque in form and exploited this to entertain, mystify and sometimes to instruct.**

Welcome to the fantasy world of Master Make-up Designer, Roy Ashton – hailed as The King of Horror. When Roy passed away on January 10, 1995, he left behind an extensive collection of his original designs, notes, and test photographs for numerous films, many of which have now achieved cult status.

Over the course of eight years, the authors have catalogued and preserved this priceless collection, gathering more and more information about Roy's innovative and enterprising work. We have interviewed dozens of Roy's colleagues, and have used their contributions throughout this book. One thing stands out – over

these eight years, we have not heard a single negative comment about this unusual gentleman. Quite the contrary. Many who knew Roy approached this work as a tribute. They asked if their eulogies could be printed.

The collection which Roy had accumulated over a lifetime of work in the British cinema proved to be an irreplaceable insight into cinema history, and Hammer Films, in particular. The collection is not complete. There are gaps.

Elizabeth Ashton accepts Roy's posthumous SOFFIA award from Barbara Shelley

Elizabeth Ashton:

"Various people over the years who had been writing books or fanzines had asked to borrow bits from Roy's collection. Not all of it was returned."

Introduction

Along with his good friend and Hammer make-up master, Phil Leakey, Roy Ashton received a posthumous lifetime achievement award from the Society of Fantastic Films in 1995. The award was presented by Barbara Shelley to Roy's wife, Mrs. Elizabeth Ashton. The following year, a small selection of Roy Ashton's and Phil Leakey's material formed the centrepiece of a major exhibition marking a century of British Cinema. The exhibition was at the National Museum of Photography, Film and Television in Bradford, England.

It soon became apparent that this collection was of immense importance, and the Museum became interested in acquiring it. They succeeded in April, 1998. This prestigious institution was able to purchase the Roy Ashton Collection with support from the National Heritage Lottery Fund. It was the first time the Fund, which exists to preserve British national treasures, had recognised the cinema industry as an important aspect of that heritage. The purchase also included items which had been used by Roy's predecessor at Hammer, Phil Leakey.

Michael Harvey (Curator of Cinematography, NMPFT):

"The special effects make-up work of Phil and Roy was crucial to the success of the Hammer Film's horror productions. The pioneering nature of their work is generally acknowledged by professionals throughout the industry... The significance of the unparalled collection of artefacts and drawings left by these two men is, that it shows in detail the development processes behind the final effects on-screen. The material presented in this book provides a unique insight into techniques that, by their very nature, would normally be surrounded by an aura of mystery."

Tom Edwards (Hammer's stills photographer):

"Roy's work was always kept top secret. The management saw to that. There had to be a mystery associated with how these creatures were produced. Roy's drawings and

Russell Wall, Roy Ashton and Bruce Sachs

photographs were fiercely protected. Most of the crew never saw the creature until the moment Roy would lead his newest creation onto the set. I remember a number of occasions when such an instance would visibly shock everyone present."

As this book goes to print, the Museum is creating a permanent archive and exhibition of this material. *Greasepaint and Gore* will serve as a guide through this

fantastic collection. We have lived with this material for eight years, and have developed both a deep affection for and intimate knowledge of it contents. Accordingly, we have had to make some very hard choices about what to include and what to leave out.

Roy only ever worked as a freelance. He was never an employee of Hammer. His contracts engaged him to apply make-up as required only on the days of shooting. His research and his designs were frequently done between engagements, as he knew that he wouldn't have the time to design during filming. On occasion, his designs were not used. Sometimes, the studio would engage someone other than Roy. He could never be secure in employment. He saved his designs, in the knowledge that he owned them, and he might find further uses for his ideas. Roy did indeed own his creations, and following legal investigations, his designs have recently been registered with the Design and Artists Copyright Society.

Before he died, Roy had been enthusiastically supportive of the *Greasepaint and Gore* project. Extensive materials were made available to us, including his own writings, notes, and taped interviews. We have had to edit all of this material for inclusion in this book. It is important to note that statements attributed here to Roy have been patchworked together from a variety of sources, in order to achieve the most coherent and engaging presentation of Roy's own words. Throughout the book, all of Roy's own contributions are printed in bold. We believe that Roy had an unusual style of expression, intertwining seriousness with a humourous twist. We hope that we have preserved the flavour of his expressions. Similarly, we have relied heavily on quoting many of those who knew and worked with Roy. Hence, there will be a wide variety of perspectives presented here. We have chosen to allow those who contributed to have their say, and the authors have tried to remain neutral. This sense of oral history, we believe, is the most appropriate and honest way to present this material.

The intriguing history unfolding in these pages will be of immense interest to horror fans world-wide. But we believe this book is an important document of British

The Ashton Collection – the centrepiece of the **Magic Behind the Screen** *exhibition at the National Museum of Photography, Film and Television in 1996.*

cinema history, and an inspiration for those contemplating a career in Roy's footsteps. While we have approached this project with a sense of sincerity and respect, we also hope that the book provides a sense of fun. It is meant to be enjoyed.

The National Museum of Photography, Film and Television now provides a permanent home to the Roy Ashton Collection

> Being freelance is never easy in any profession, but it is especially true of the film industry. I have sometimes been in the unfortunate position of wondering just where sufficient money was coming from to pay my bills. Sometimes, I envy those bowler-hatted civil servants who seem to march on without departing from a fairly straightforward line in one particular career. But when I stop to consider what those people feel like when they arrive at the end of their 40 years of service, I wonder if they are happy with their lot! Perhaps even without the security, it hasn't been a bad old life after all, singing opera and making monsters!

The Roy Ashton Story

Much of what follows has been adapted from the unpublished notes of: *An Autobiography* by Roy Ashton. Roy described this work in a letter to his friend Uwe Sommerlad, dated 14 September 1990 as: "...an attempt to explain one or two things about my adventures here and there."

My name is Howard Roy Ashton. I was born in Perth, Western Australia on the 17 April 1909. My life has always been associated with drawing and designing and with music. I sang for many years in Opera. I was a founder member of the English Opera Group and I have appeared more than 3,000

times as a soloist. I have sometimes worked with musical colleagues simultaneously as performer and supervisor of their make-up. When I returned to films, I went to Bray Studios for a stint of some 35 films, mostly Hammer Horrors. When it was suggested that I should record a history of my life, "Goodness!", I thought. Who might be interested in my recollections of music and artistic matters? However, looking through my sketch books and diaries I reflected on all the marvellous people it has been my privilege to know in private and professional life. I pondered on the happy coincidences and the tragic events. I tried to connect in my mind some of the strange twists and turns of fate that have occurred and how they helped shape the person I have become. I will not say that my life has not been without its share of problems. At times it has been very difficult indeed to know where my next step should be taken. Yet, I know the development of character is gained only through diligence and the overcoming of difficulties. So in my eighty first year with pen in hand I will begin my story in those terribly anxious times when water was at a premium, when gold mining was in its infancy, and goats were the only company that my three brothers and I ever knew!

Roy Ashton's Early Life in Australia

My mother was Anne (née Morris), my Father: Howard White Ashton. My earliest memories of Father are of him standing behind two barrels and a plank. This was the makeshift counter on which he weighed gold nuggets in a huge pair of scales. Dad was in charge of the local bank in Menzies. In fact, he was the youngest man ever to become manager of a branch in Western Australia. I have been told that he was considered quite brilliant in handling difficult clients. I suppose that was why he was chosen to cultivate accounts amongst prospectors in the last great Australian gold rush. Most of the makeshift settlements in which we lived have since disappeared. Their names may linger in the memory of old folk but they never graced a map. These were pioneer days comparable to the old American West. Some men toiled for years and died in poverty whilst others literally stumbled across vast fortunes in gold and opals, buried a few inches beneath the ground.

If Father had a great head for figures, Mother was an extraordinary singer and pianist. In her youth, Dame Nellie Melba wanted to bring my Mother to

Young Roy Ashton

England with her opera company. But Dame Nellie was very strict about certain things, she told Mother "I'm not taking any married girls on tour with me. They are more trouble than they are worth!" And so before Mother married Dad there was a very hard choice for her to make. She could either pursue a professional career in music or marry the man she loved. Luckily for me that she chose the latter. They must have been extremely hard conditions in which a young couple tried to raise a family. There were four sons: Neil, Alan, Perth and the youngest, myself. Each of us bore the first name of Howard in respect of my Father's maternal family, so were known by our middle names. My grandmother was Emma Howard. She was a milliner and lived in Stony Stratford, England, before marrying a vicar and emigrating to Australia. My father's family came from Penzance.

They were very primitive conditions indeed in those far distant days on the gold fields. The miners were lovely kindly men. They were so considerate. "Take all the crockery down from the shelves, Missus!" they would yell in through the doorway to our home. "We're going to do some blasting!" My mother was a hardworking soul and a wonderful companion to us all. She would wipe her hands on her apron and duly remove all the pots and pans down from the dresser. Bricks and mortar were a far away luxury. For many years we lived in 'canvas humpies' – this was the local name for large canvas tents. Later whilst living in the wheat belt, Father presented us with a wooden bungalow, surrounded by a large veranda. It was on the veranda where we spent most of our time. Sometimes violent thunderstorms appeared in the middle of the night. Lightning dazzled us and raindrops the size of golf balls peppered down onto the corrugated iron roofs. What a racket the rain made. When this first happened we all jumped out of bed with a terrible fright. It was the end of any thoughts of sleeping for the rest of that night I can assure you.

When my family returned to the big city I won a scholarship to Perth

Modern School, which was the best of the day visiting schools at that time. I was mad about sport, art and especially music.

During the Depression most of the young men of my acquaintance lacked jobs. I certainly did for a couple of years and tried to remedy the situation by writing to a firm of commercial artists. They offered a correspondence course of self discipline. I trained my hand and eye to copy objects, design elementary lettering and learn about composition. My idea was to become a professional artist but this experience was not enough to find a steady job.

My brothers were fortunate in that they had already left home in search of their fortunes. Alan became a civil engineer in the South Sea Islands. Later, he returned to Australia and helped construct the Orde River Dam in the Northern Territory. Neil went to New York and trained to be a chiropractor developing a successful practice in Singapore, London and Sydney. Eventually, brother Perth was to follow Father into banking.

I began my working life by serving formal articles in architecture. After two years toiling in the Government's Public Works Department, I left to become an illustrator in a commercial firm of block makers and designers. Suddenly the Great Depression arrived and there was no work. I was made redundant with another young man on the principle of 'last in' post being the 'first out'. We got together as commercial artists and we scraped a living of sorts.

I realised I was at a cross-roads in my life. I decided that my destiny lay in another country so in the spring of 1932, at the age of 23, I decided to journey to England in search of my fortune. This is the way that I came. I travelled as a member of the crew of a tramp steamer.

Father persuaded the ship's master to take me. In addition to the cargo, they carried about four passengers. So Father argued, "If you have passengers you've got to have a purser". He paid the ship's master about £100 and loaned me a further £100 to cover my living expenses. The adventure of a lifetime had begun.

The Long Voyage

The first impression of waking up on that first morning at sea was the immensity of the waves roundabout this cockleshell of a ship. The waves seemed like mountains. From crest to crest they were immense, towering way above the deck across which I staggered about on, in wonder and amazement.

Occasionally great whales would lift themselves out of the waves and crash down with great force. Large shoals of dolphins would swim alongside and race in front of the prow, keeping station with the ship's movement.

I had plenty of time to write and I recorded all of these things in long letters home to my dear parents. However, I had no idea when I would be able to post them. It took the ship three weeks to cross the sea to our first port of call, Durban, in South Africa. Our stay was sufficient only to fill up the bunkers with coal. Then around the Cape of Good Hope we travelled to Dakar in Senegal and on through the Straits of Gibraltar. The Mediterranean, which I expected to be land locked and therefore calm, was exactly the opposite. A raging gale funnelled down from the Pyrenees, forced us to heave to for three days and nights, with waves smashing over everything from bow to stern. When the storm subsided we went along the coasts of France and Italy en route for Livorno. Whilst the crew discharged our cargo of bulk wheat, I had made the round-trip between Livorno and Pisa by push bike. It had been a long journey and I felt quite tired. But I had a passion to drink in as much of this ancient culture as my short time would allow. I ran between an army of Renaissance sculptures, scribbling down sketches and notes along the way. I paused for breathe inside the Cathedral in which Galileo had watched the gigantic candelabrum swinging from the ceiling and had set him speculating on the properties of pendulums. The famous leaning tower was another curiosity that occupied my interest. I climbed to the top and settled down to enjoy the extraordinary view. I suppose when one comes to think about things, learning and the blossoming of ideas is not confined to any one time or nationality. It is a continuous world of stimulus really, which starts people thinking along fresh paths of intellectual discovery.

When I returned to the vessel I learnt that we were very soon to return to England to discharge the remainder of our cargo at a port on the Bristol channel. At last I was about to set foot on the shores of the motherland, my ultimate destination. I wondered what fate had in store for me there? Although I had certain skills in both drawing and music I couldn't have guessed that in the years to follow I would be able to apply my talents, such as they are, to the business of earning a living.

The first place I called after quitting the tramp steamer on the Bristol Channel was the YMCA. There, two letters of welcome awaited me from my parents. I will admit that my eyes filled with tears when I received them. They expressed all the love and kindness possible. I read and reread them wondering if they had received my letters written aboard ship. I found a room in Kings Cross and stayed there for about a week. My secret wish, in fact, was to study music: I always had a great love of it. Besides, I practically grew up with it as my father was an amateur musician and my mother a professional. I did have aspirations of making my way as a singer. I had a certain degree of training in singing: I had lessons privately, and even had a chance of a scholarship at the Royal College School of Music, though without very much hope of making a living out of it. As it happened, I looked into it but I didn't take it up. Consequently, I concentrated on the art side. I found myself standing on the pavement outside The Central School of Arts and Crafts. In I went and enrolled as a student in several classes. Then one day in 1933, by chance an advertisement pinned to a notice board at the School of Arts and Crafts caught my eye. The proclamation announced that the Gaumont British Film Corporation were looking for a small number of apprentices to embark on a new training programme in film make-up. This apprenticeship would pay a regular fee of about two pounds a week. Interviews took place at Gaumont British Film Studios at Shepherd's Bush. There were a number of small tests to decide the suitability of each applicant. In addition to rather tricky questions about how to research historical details there were a number of proficiency tests in drawing. After lunch, to my delight I was invited to join the course.

The Making Of A Make-up Man

For the next five years I would walk from my flat on Mill Bank close to the Tate Gallery alongside the River Thames and take a bus to Gainsborough Studios in Islington. I was apprenticed to Norman Rosenthal. Herr Rosenthal was on secondment from the famed UFA Studios in Berlin. He was a key 'Maskenbilder' in the German Expressionist Film Movement and later he took charge of the Schiller Theatre also in Berlin.

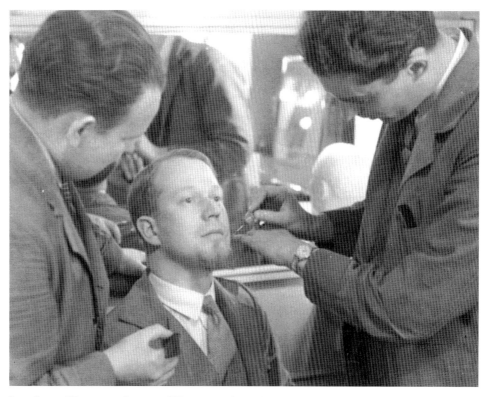

The tasks performed by make-up trainees in the 1930s were much the same as they are today. We had to learn to prepare the artists' faces and develop skills in shading and applying highlights. I also had to learn to make hair pieces. I learned to make beards and sew the wig mounts and make coiffures and so on. We were given hair which was just shorn off and looked unspeakable in every way. A lot of it came from the Ukraine... We had to sort it out into its different colours and textures, wash it, then manipulate it with a little hook through a mesh. We had to be instructed how to put it in, how to fashion it, curl it, make toupees and crowns etc., so that we could exactly imitate the natural shape of peoples' hair. I also had to teach myself to sew, of which I had no experience at all. To make a wig you need to do very neat and precise sewing... I sat there for hours handling a needle, as I was determined to show those German chaps that I could do it.

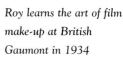

Above:
Roy learns the art of film make-up at British Gaumont in 1934

Elizabeth Ashton:

"Out of his meagre wages as an apprentice, Roy saved enough to send back to his father the £200 he originally borrowed to come to England. This was a fantastic achievement when you think about it. Roy said he was living on bread and cheese during his apprenticeship. He didn't eat much at all and as a result ran himself down terribly. The Germans were very hard task masters and at one point they said Roy wasn't quick enough and he was afraid he wouldn't be kept on. He was told to make a wig and he had to stay up all night to finish it. All around the hairline he threaded each hair through the hair lace, one hair at a time. It was very tedious but it was fascinating watching him work and make all the hairs go the same way. One of the things he used to hate the most in this early stage was that the make-up department at Gainsborough used to get regular deliveries of boxes of long human hair from Russia.

The Roy Ashton Story

The first thing Roy had to do after washing it was "top and tail" it. Human hair is like a feather: it has a scales like a fish. He had to find the right direction in which to brush the hair for cutting and styling. Sometimes, Roy would find pieces of skin attached to the hair and even portions of human scalps. It was a horribly messy business. Sometimes the hair was matted with blood. Much later, Roy realised that this hair had been taken from the corpses of people who had been executed. After this realisation Roy really hated working with human hair. He didn't mind cutting someone else's hair but he hated touching pieces of hair that had been cut. At home if any stray hair was left in the bath or washing basin, Roy couldn't stand it. I think that his experience at Gainsborough all came flashing back to him."

Above and below:
Further tutelage at British
Gaumont in 1934

It took a lot to prove to Rosenthal that we apprentices were all quite serious in our hopes of becoming make-up artists. But once he was convinced

of our intentions he was as good as gold and did his best to teach us everything he knew about the make-up craft. What are the attributes needed to make a good make-up person? What you do require is patience, and devotion to the work, good health and the ability to work long hours. Drawing and modelling are a great help and you must also know how to handle hair. A make-up artist should be able to make hairpieces even if he or she hasn't the time to do so. We do still make them in individual cases from scratch. We certainly design them. Nowadays though, we use all types of specially prepared human and animal hair. I have no preference, but for very rapid work, I normally use creped wool. Herr Rosenthal was extremely thorough in his training and we covered a wide number of techniques. But prosthetics were scarcely in use in those days. It was only subsequently when I went to Hammer Films that I began to experiment with such properties, and casting and modelling plastic noses and all that sort of thing. Today there is so much happening in connection with prosthetic appliances anyone who has a knowledge of chemistry has a great advantage over his associates.

Roy's Gainsborough Years.

Gainsborough Pictures was to become most famous as the home of stylish Regency melodramas, starring Margaret Lockwood, James Mason, Stewart Grainger and Phyllis Calvert, two hot blooded examples being *The Man in Grey* (1943) and *The Wicked Lady* (1945). However, these glory days were still to come as part of the blossoming Rank Organisation. For during the 1930s, with production facilities at Islington, Gainsborough Pictures was more synonymous with the Aldwich film farces, starring Tom Walls, Ralph Lynn and Robertson Hare, and the Will Hay comedies

such as *Windbag The Sailor* (1936), *Oh Mr Porter!* (1937) and *Convict 99* (1938). Although studio head Edward Black did produce occasional blockbusters such as Alfred Hitchcock's *The Lady Vanishes* (1938) and Carol Reed's *Bank Holiday* (1938), the emphasis was on low budget products with dependable box-office performance. Gainsborough Pictures was an excellent training ground for up and coming British filmmakers who, like Roy Ashton, were eventually to make their way to Bray Studios. This influential group included film director Terence Fisher, editor James Needs, stills photographer Johnny Jay, and Gainsborough Girls Hazel Court and Diana Dors. Roy Ward Baker, director of the classic Titanic drama, *A Night To Remember* (1958) was also at Gainsborough and went on to direct many Hammer and Amicus features.

Roy Ward Baker:

"Edward Black was a very nice man. I owe him a great debt. He was very kind and down to earth and in a way, very indulgent to young people who were thrashing about all the time. Len Harris started at Gainsborough as well. Len was one of the gang. We were all in our late teens and used to congregate in the camera room on the quiet and play pontoon for pennies. Miraculously I worked at Gainsborough for six years and had two weeks paid holiday a year. But other than that, I was never out of work. That is why I had such a solid background as an apprentice. I worked on 38 pictures at Gainsborough. It was six years to the day when I joined the army. It was a pity that more notice wasn't taken of Gainsborough Pictures at the time. It was always over-shadowed by Gaumont British. But they were making the prestige pictures whilst we were producing the money making stuff."

Above:
Moore Marriott from the
Will Hay comedies

We all learned a lot working at Gainsborough. Billy Partleton was extremely helpful in the make-up department. Whilst Herr Rosenthal attended to the stars of the picture, it was our task to get the other performers ready. To remember all the productions that I have worked on is a bit difficult. The first film in which I can claim direct responsibility in designing and making the wigs is _Tudor Rose_ (1936).

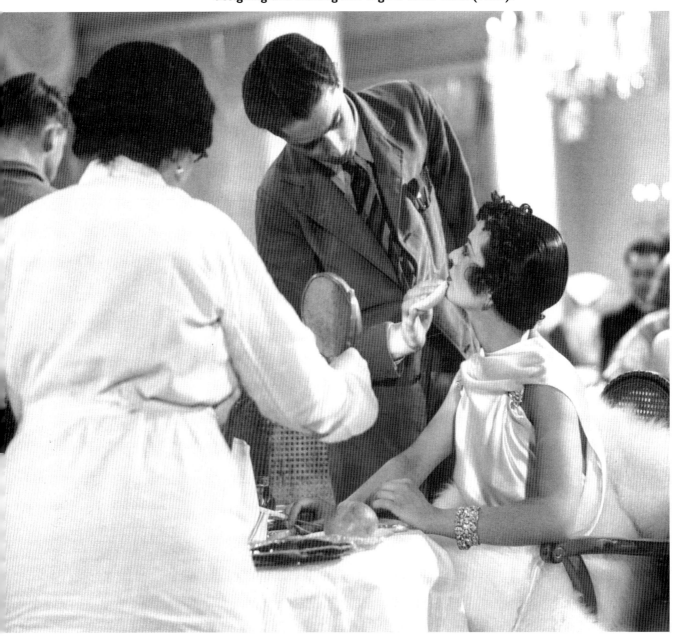

....

Above:

Roy applies make-up on Gainsborough's Jack of All Trades

Roy Ward Baker:

"I was third assistant director at the time of _Tudor Rose_. What really fascinated me was up till that time Gainsborough had been making simple thrillers and comedies. They were very good but _Tudor Rose_ was the first serious drama with top rank actors in that I had ever worked on. John Mills was already an established leading man and the rest of the cast were amazing: Cedric Hardwicke, Ben Franklyn Davis, Felix Aylmer and Sybil Thorndyke were in it too."

I really did *Tudor Rose* with a colleague of mine called John Wilcox. As a challenge, before it was shot, six extras were brought in. The producer – I believe it was Ted Black – and director Robert Stevenson said: "If you fellows can make a satisfactory job on those characters who are Tudor historic personages, then you can do the film." So, I went to the British Museum and purchased some reproductions of Holbein drawings, which were appropriate for the era. I made wigs and beards and so on, put them on these people and showed them to Stevenson and the producer, who agreed. They gave us the basis of the design and said we could go ahead.

Left:
Sir Cedric Hardwicke as appeared in Tudor Rose

Terence Fisher acted as an assistant cutter on *Tudor Rose*. Quite a coincidence, isn't it? Later I came to work quite often with old Terry, such a nice man... Having been a cutter he knew exactly what each separate shot was going to look like on the screen... They also had a couple of writers at Gainsborough, Launder and Gilliat, who have since developed into producers and directors themselves. There was another man, Vetchinsky, an art director: he has done numerous pictures and is still in the trade. And they had a gag man, whose name was Val Guest. He was a gag man providing jokes and funny stories for the Will Hay comedies at Gainsborough.

Val Guest:

"For years Gainsborough kept Lime Grove and British Gaumont afloat. They paid for what the other studios lost. Eventually when the Lime Grove studios at Shepherd's Bush went out of business, Gainsborough moved in and took it over. It was fabulous to work there: like a big family, rather like the next big family I worked for who were the Hammer people."

Val Guest eventually became a noted screenwriter/director and was responsible for the smooth economic production of many Hammer comedies and influential thrillers such as *The Quatermass Experiment* (1955). Roy Ashton's first solo effort *Tudor Rose* was helmed by Robert Stevenson later to direct prolifically and almost exclusively for Walt Disney. In 1936 Stevenson was just as highly regarded by Gainsborough Pictures. As proof of this, Stevenson was chosen to direct Boris Karloff in *The Man Who Changed His Mind*. This was the first film that the Hollywood star made in his native England that year, (the other being the disappointing *Juggernaut*). However, fresh from his triumph repeating his role as the Monster in *Bride of Frankenstein* (1935), Karloff was at the height of his powers and a major marketing coup for Gaumont British. Despite all of the project's potential, exhibition problems in the UK for Horror films meant that "a Karloff film" was difficult to promote. Local councils threatened to ban *The Man Who Changed His Mind* even before production was underway and there were rumours of Gaumont British cancelling Karloff's contract. In the light of these production problems, and his status as a major Hollywood star, was Karloff a difficult performer to work with?

Oh No, I should say not! Boris Karloff was a lovely person. His real name was William Henry Pratt, although in private Mr. Karloff preferred to be called Harry. He was delighted to be back in England. An avid cricket fan he insisted on being kept up to date on the latest Test scores. This was my first

Horror Film on the theme of eternal youth. It was about a Mad Doctor who creates a machine that makes the transmigration of the human soul possible. We had long discussions about how Mr. Karloff saw his character. I designed and made a rather severe steel grey wig in *The Man Who Changed His Mind*. This arose from the incident where he had an extra shot to do after the film

24

had been completed. As he had his hair cut in the meantime, they ordered me to make a wig to match it as it had been before, which was a great privilege. I took the train to Hurley, out of London, where he had taken up his residence, and measured him up. Having returned to the studio to report there, I went up to the warehouse and bought a couple of ounces of hair that had the right colour, and patiently made the wig. At first he said: "Well, I don't know, I'm not keen!" But on second thoughts he admitted it was a good job, so we carried on. Apart from that my memory is a little bit vague about the actual shooting of the film. Boris Karloff was a most charming man. As a matter of fact, he gave me a five pound note after we had finished. In England, in those days, a bank note was a piece of high quality linen: you didn't see too many around in the places where I was. I stared at it and stammered: "Oh God, look at this! It's marvellous !" I should have asked him to autograph it, it would have been worth a lot more now! I know Mr. Karloff had the greatest admiration for Jack Pierce. He was one of the great pioneers. I think all make-up artists feel the same. I never miss an

....

Below:
"Roy Ashton doing the make-up? Oh dear"

opportunity to look at stills of his work and marvel at his skill in handling the materials which were then generally in use. His Frankenstein's creature was a landmark in Horror film make-up. Of course much development has taken place with the materials at our disposal, especially in the fields of plastics and adhesives. Rubber appliances have also much developed. It is a pity that film companies are not on a permanent basis as in the old Gainsborough days. Today's spasmodic production system means that there are periods of

unemployment for make-up artists and a wasting of much stock, poor continuity of research, application and management of specialised skills.

The film work that followed *The Man Who Changed His Mind* during the remainder of Roy's tenure at Gainsborough were relatively unchallenging. Roy had once quipped to Will Hay, "Where there's a Will there's a Hay." A greetings card from Hay to Roy retorted, "Where there's a Will there's a wig." *Dr. Syn* (1937) however, proved a notable exception to the rule. The lead was played by veteran actor George Arliss, who had learned his craft as a member of the Arthur 'A.J.' Jefferson Players in the North East of England. Incidentally, 'A.J.'s' son was to follow Arliss to Hollywood and eventually find success as comedian Stan Laurel. *Dr. Syn* was to be George Arliss' last film.

Above:
The original Dr. Syn

Roy Ward Baker:

"George Arliss was charming but he was a dyed in the wool old fashioned 'ack-tor' of the Edwardian period. He had started in movies in the Silent days with Warner's making those potted biographies like Wellington and Disraeli. I don't think that he attempted Napoleon, but he did most of them! Then lo and behold! when sound came in they asked him to go back to Warner's and remake them all. He came back over to Britain to do *Dr. Syn*. He was extremely accurate and punctilious. He stepped onto the set at 9 a.m. and expected to start work straight away. He was fully made-up, dressed and ready with the words and all that. Well, he'd written a lot of them himself anyway. At 4 p.m. his butler, a man named Jenner, came onto the stage. He would bow slightly to George Arliss and say 'Tea is ready sir!' George Arliss went off the set to have his tea and that was that for the day. He worked like that for five days a week for four weeks and that was the contract. No negotiations. I think he was paid about £4000, which was a lot of money.

26

Of course if you are doing one in four weeks, there are 52 weeks in a year and so you can work up a hefty gross if you put your nose down. But he was an interesting character and nice enough."

Based on the novel "Moonfleet" by Roger (the brother of Sybil) Thorndyke, *Dr. Syn* is a suspenseful historical thriller, a tale of pirates, and smugglers with undertones of horror that became amplified in Hammer's reworking of the same material as *Captain Clegg* (1962). I once wrote a sequel to the tale for Tony Hinds. But he wasn't persuaded to produce it, although they were keen to find a successor for their version of *Dr. Syn* at the time. Of course, *Moonfleet* was made by MGM with Stewart Granger - but it didn't bear much resemblance to the original story.

The Artist Wore Khaki

I left Gainsborough Pictures and I worked as a freelance for London Films in Denham, which was Alexander Korda's stronghold at the time. There, first of all, I worked on *The Rope* (1938), and then with Luis Trenker on *The Challenge* (1938) which was about mountain climbers. Then I moved over to a film named *Prison Without Bars* (1938), with Corinne Luchaire. This was the first film where I was in charge of make-up. Alas! This independence didn't last long. I remember the very day the war broke out. I was actually busy in the Denham studios on a Sunday as we heard the sirens go. Merle Oberon and Alexander Korda were seeking shelter in the basement, where the generators and all those kinds of

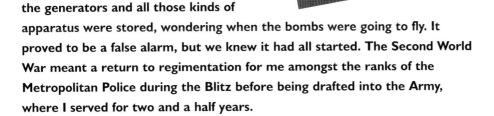

apparatus were stored, wondering when the bombs were going to fly. It proved to be a false alarm, but we knew it had all started. The Second World War meant a return to regimentation for me amongst the ranks of the Metropolitan Police during the Blitz before being drafted into the Army, where I served for two and a half years.

Elizabeth Ashton:

"I met Roy at the Royal Academy of Music. He got a scholarship there whilst in the Police Force. Working 24 hours on, 24 hours off, he came to the Academy. Roy went into the Army and we never communicated. I went to a concert at Wigmore Hall and in the interval I met Roy on the first day of a week's leave. He asked me to play the piano for him and we arranged to meet at Gloucester Road station. I was going to go to Baker Street, and get a train on the Circle Line to Gloucester Road station. I waited for half an hour and there was no train. Then a message came on the tannoy 'We are very sorry. We have discovered a bomb on the line. The Circle Line is closed.' I thought 'Oh dear! I haven't got a telephone number for Roy. I can't get in touch. He

27

doesn't know where I live. He'll have to get in touch with me at the Academy.' I walked back across the platform bridge and Roy was walking towards me. He was always half an hour early. He'd arrived at the Gloucester Road station, found out there was a bomb on the line and walked in the hope of meeting me. 'Come along me old mate!' he said and took my hand. I thought 'Oh! I've come home' and that clinched it."

My first Army posting was to learn the intricacies of Radar. I instructed others in the tracking of enemy planes for several months. Then one day I was sent to a selection board with the idea of organising musical entertainment for the troops. I had frequently arranged makeshift concert parties in my spare time and wanted to make this my full-time occupation. The result of the interview was an order to forge foreign ration documents. I had hardly settled into my new post when I was put to work at the Natural History Museum. Within a certain gallery was a team of men working to construct weapons of a doubtful appearance, but extremely efficient in killing people. There were all sorts of gadgets: exploding fountain pens and umbrella's which fired poison darts. Upon these secret weapons I was required to lecture to fellows from other countries with scrambled egg all over their caps.

Right:
Army days...

Far Right:
Roy appears on stage with
Winifred Radford
as members of The
Intimate Opera

The secret department in which Roy worked was headed by Charles Fraser Smith. Its purpose was to create concealed weapons and gadgets to assist undercover operatives serving behind enemy lines in occupied Europe. Ian Fleming closely observed this very special research and development unit and later immortalised their activities in his James Bond novels. It would have amused Roy to have been considered as a prototype for the eccentric and unflappable 'Q': the man in the white coat who introduces Bond to his arsenal of fantastic weapons before each adventure.

I used to discourse most learnedly, even though most of the time I must admit I didn't have the faintest idea what I was talking about. Suddenly, the war was over and the unit's sugar ration disappeared. At the same time the officer in charge miraculously discovered sugar in his urine and was demobbed, due to "ill health". I was a Lance Corporal and left in charge of the exhibition. At one time I was required to entertain her Royal Highness

Queen Mary and the two Princesses Elizabeth and Margaret to afternoon tea,
along with Lord Willoughby de Broke. I rushed around to Lyons Corner
House and borrowed a set of cups and saucers, and purchased some buns.
Lord Willoughby de Broke spent most of his time relating how he had
persuaded a bomber to bring some fresh eggs all the way from Belgium to

some airfield in Britain. The little Princesses were very interested in all the
implements of destruction that the galleries held. They were a murderous lot,
I do assure you. Not the Princesses of course, but the implements of

destruction. Everyday some edict would be circulated from the army. One said that anyone who had an unfinished scholarship at University could get an early discharge. I had a year to go on my scholarship at the **Royal Academy of Music**. That was October 1945 and I was out by January 1946. They gave me a terrible pair of trousers for my 'demob' suit but I was out of the Army and seriously back in music. These were some of the happiest years of my life.

Roy's Career in Music

I must confess my principal love is music and it was my deep passion to become a singer which fired my musical ambitions. My mother was a very successful singer and I believe she instilled this great love of music within me. So many times would she play my brothers and myself to sleep and awaken us with music. Even now I find solace in fine compositions by composers who know their craft. Those who share this passion will understand what I mean when I say that God gave music to mankind for their joy and upliftment.

During my five years' apprenticeship in the Film Industry I had never ceased to practice music. With a regular wage I had started payments on a modest piano more in hope than in the expectation that it would ever become mine. But after three years it really did belong to me and became my most treasured possession. When I look back now I see it was certainly a test of my tenacity to become a performer. Make-up required dedicated hours of study and application, far and away beyond that usually required to earn a living. Yet somehow God gave me the stamina I needed. I would rise very early in the morning and practice. Arriving home late in the evening I made a meal, then set about my musical studies. It was a very busy time indeed, but I suppose such experience of life is necessary in order to have sufficient self reliance. One needs an inner strength to face such trials, to make the difference between earning a living or merely existing. Having tasted the sadness of unemployment I did not wish to suffer that difficulty again. So I worked hard in learning the craft of make-up, an occupation that I did not really enjoy but which I used as a stepping stone to my real love – that of music.

In 1947 in the old days of Grand Opera they used to have Entr'Acte – 'in-between-the-acts' short pieces. In the interval, two or three people would come on and do some other little opera by Mozart, Dibden and Purcell. Producer Geoffrey Dunn got together Winifred Radford and Frederick Woodhouse, and started a company called *Intimate Opera*. We would travel all around the country touring for a week doing three operas a night. I sang more than two thousand performances of these little operas. I thoroughly enjoyed this activity, interspersed with engagements to perform at various Cathedrals and musical centres. Eventually I became a member of *The English Opera Group*. Once I became established as principal operatic tenor at Glyndebourne and Covent Garden I moved about all over Britain and the Continent.

Composer Benjamin Britten described the objectives of *The English Opera Group* as: "dedicated to the creation of new works…capable of attracting new audiences by being toured all over the country." The scale of the new venture was to be kept as small as possible - since it was only thus that "the principles of high quality in singing, musicianship and preparation can be reconciled with the regular performance of new works. The time has come when England, which has always depended on a repertory of foreign works can create its own operas... It is part of the group's purpose to encourage young composers to write for the operatic stage...".

Roy Ashton joined *The English Opera Group* in December 1947. He understudied Peter Pears and created the role of The Mayor in *Albert Herring*.

In its first three years *The English Opera Group* had toured its productions of *The Rape of Lucretia*, *Albert Herring* and *The Beggar's Opera* across Holland, Belgium, Switzerland, Denmark and Norway. Both *The Rape of Lucretia* and *Albert Herring* were included in *The English Opera Group*'s tour abroad to the International Festival at Scheveningen, the Stadsschouwburg in Amsterdam and the Lucerne International Festival. During their visit to

Roy designed his own make-up and costumes for his role in Purcell's opera **Don Quixote**

Switzerland, a concert was given at Zurich. Back in England, they gave ten opera performances at Covent Garden and toured to Newcastle upon Tyne, Bournemouth and Oxford before dispersing for the winter. *Peter Grimes* reached the Scala, Milan, the Opera House, Paris in 1947, and The Metropolitan Opera House, New York, the following year. It was during the first tour of *Albert Herring* that Roy and Elizabeth Cooper were married.

Elizabeth Ashton:

"It's funny! I remember the very first performance of *Albert Herring* was at Cheltenham Town Hall in 1947. I sat in the very front row. I knew the opera backwards because I taught Roy his part. So as each person was coming in I knew what was going to happen. I started to laugh out loud. When they go to the first performance of a new opera, the audience doesn't know what to expect. They may be going to see a piece like *Billy Budd* which is very serious. But I knew that *Albert Herring* was a comic opera. I also was privy to what had been going on back stage. I knew that Roy's costume was too tight, a split had appeared right up the back and his whole costume was held together with two safety pins. So I was laughing fit to bring the house down. Benjamin Britten went round the back and rubbed his hands together in glee that things were going so well. He said 'There's a marvellous woman sitting in the front row. She's understood the tone from the first act!' Roy said 'Sorry Ben. That's my fiancée.'"

In my operatic days my technical skill with make-up had served me well. Often my stage colleagues were surprised by my ability to fashion my character make-up and create my own properties. On occasion I also found I could help them with their own portrayals. There was a smallish company called Festival Opera and I appeared with my wife Elizabeth.

Elizabeth Ashton:

"There was a lovely old chap who had been in the D'Oyle Carte with his wife for many years singing Gilbert and Sullivan operas. Of course in *Faust* Roy starts as an old man with bald head, whiskers, and all the rest of it and transforms into this young man after selling his soul to the devil. This old performer came up to Roy in rehearsals and said 'My dear fellow, if you have any problems with your make-up just ask me. It's no problem!'. Roy said, 'Thanks. I think I'll be able to manage.'

The financial rewards in the late 40s and early 50s cannot be compared with the inflated fees that certain artists receive today. Sometimes we felt ourselves fortunate if our expenses were met. However although it did not provide fortunes for us, it certainly did give us enormous satisfaction. It is my personal feeling that to perform fine works with splendid colleagues endowed with great gifts and an abundant sense of humour cannot be equalled. Nothing can compare with the thrill of appearing before a great gathering, of hearing the thunder of the applause delivered to a sincere artist. There is of course the lasting pleasure in the realisation of work well done.

Returning To Film

I never left NATKE (The National Association of Theatre and Kine Employees) and that's how I got work as a make-up artist in the film industry. It was a good thing too because by 1952 there was very little singing work available. It was a very sad ending, but with the formation of broadcasting companies, there was a winding up of touring companies in opera. This was

chiefly because oratorio societies and music clubs, smaller opera clubs had spent all their money in 1951 for The Festival of Britain. The financial rewards of working in the film industry were naturally far greater. But before any engagement was undertaken the bargaining took place. I came to hate these formalities as I firmly believe the labourer is worthy of his hire. In one sense the life of an opera performer was much less hazardous, for the arrangement of fees were carried out long in advance of the performance by correspondence. Despite my reservations it was not long before I found openings with the major film companies. The thought of remaining at home and commuting to a nearby studio soon became a vain idea. I moved about the world even more than when I was performing opera full-time. A film company may move to any part of the world in search of a satisfactory location. You are never quite certain of a company's movements. But you are generally housed in elegant places because you are usually placed in close proximity to the principal actors.

Elizabeth Ashton:

"When Roy wasn't working he would stay at home practising and learning new operas. He learned the whole of Verdi's *Othello* at one time. From time to time we would sing professionally together. We sang *Elijah* together at Ely Cathedral and Verdi's *Requiem* at Putney. Roy was always ready to return to opera. He organised singing work well in advance and liked to keep his two professions – that of freelance make-up man and opera singer completely separate."

Roy Ashton generally sang in the winter and worked on feature films in the summer. But in 1954 because as he put it: "In the Music lark you're never at home. You're all over the blessed place" – he decided that more regular film work would provide a more profitable future.

Yet, even then, I continued to perform occasionally. I recollect getting a job in one production which I combined with singing in the evening. The next day I arrived at the studio with an early morning call, when the soprano from the previous night turned up there and saw me in the make-up room. She said: "What the heck are you doing here?" "I am working here," I replied. She couldn't believe it. Still I went on and made her up, collected my fee and that was that. Sometimes people were asking me what I was going to be, singer or a make-up man: anyway, it sorted itself out.

Working with Orson Welles

Elizabeth Ashton:

"Roy was still singing when he got the chance to do *Mr. Arkadin* (1955) with Orson Welles. We got this phone call from Stanley Hall, of Wig Creations, saying that Welles was having difficulties with his toupee."

Stanley asked me would I care to go out to Madrid and see what the trouble was. What I had understood was that the toupee – it wasn't a full one, but an appliance to give the impression of having the hair "en brosse" –

had split or broken. After close examination, I found it was not damaged but that Welles had been trying to put it on himself... Now, the grease had not been powdered on the top as it should have been and this resulted in a very thick coating on the hair lace, becoming most apparent in the photography. Similarly with the beard: it had not been cleaned after use, thus losing its form and vitality. I was able to put that right also, freshening up the moustaches and all the rest of it. He then asked me to stay. So I remained with him until the shooting was finished, though I had imagined that I would only have to go out for a couple of days! Some hope!

Elizabeth Ashton:

"Roy told me that Orson had a very small nose and always insisted on having false noses which had to be moulded and stuck on. When Roy was asked to stay out in Spain he was well aware of Orson Welles' reputation. Roy agreed but stipulated that if his salary wasn't paid exactly on time he would leave. Roy was at the Hilton in Madrid and he had a communication from *The English Opera Group* which I forwarded out to him. They had telephoned him in England, before he started on *Mr. Arkadin.* They wanted him to perform *Albert Herring* and Roy said that he had got this film work lined up. The person on the telephone asked if he'd got a contract and when Roy answered 'No' He said 'Well it's only a verbal agreement. You don't have to keep that.' 'I certainly do' Roy replied. 'I've given my word'. That cooked his goose with *The English Opera Group*, but so many of these people were like this. They demanded a 100% of your time and couldn't understand that Roy needed to make a living. When Roy had been out a week he contacted the producer Louis Dolivet about his wages. The producer said 'Could we leave it a little while?' Roy said 'I'm going to ring my wife and she is going to go to your solicitors in London to collect my wages on Thursday morning'. He told me how much he was owed and I went to the offices. At first they refused payment, so I said 'In that case I have to phone my husband in Spain to return to England because he will not stay.' That meant that the film wouldn't get made and they wouldn't get paid. So reluctantly they paid me what was owed. This happened every week Roy was out there. He was the only person in the whole film who ever got paid anything. Presumably the rest of the cast and crew had their hotel bills paid and that was all."

I found Orson Welles a very amusing man, who used to laugh very much. A lot of people consider his unpredictability a bit hard to take, yet I thought he was particularly funny, constantly regaling us with his stories which were very often told against himself. As for the false nose business. Orson's own nose is not a very big one and as he grew increasingly massive in size the disproportion came to be more and more exaggerated and difficult to attach to his face. But despite the heat, we managed.

Elizabeth Ashton:

"Roy said Orson Welles always insisted that he had the best of everything. During the production, the company had to go to Munich and they couldn't find a hotel that would have him. This was because Orson had stayed in all of the hotels there at one time or another and never paid his bills. Apparently, he would only work when he felt like it. For instance, Orson was very temperamental. One day he was in make-up and a barber arrived to cut his hair and Orson didn't want him there for some reason, so he screamed and shouted at the barber until he ran away. Roy didn't know what to do as he was such an unruffled person. He liked to be calm and collected."

Roy provided authentic period touches to a wide variety of movies including *Captain Horatio Hornblower RN* (1951) and *Moulin Rouge* (1952). In 1956, Roy had his first taste of working on exploitation films with the little seen, *Fire Maidens from Outer Space*.

Then came *The Whole Truth* (1958), for Walton Studios. "The latter was a murder mystery directed by John Guillermin, starring Stewart Granger, Donna Reed and

George Sanders. There was nothing out of the ordinary on that, all regular make-ups." Roy recalled. He was also to provide chilling character make-up for the gripping war drama *Sea Of Sand* (1958) starring Richard Attenborough and John Mills. Roy first worked with Richard Attenborough on *Dunkirk* (1958) an Ealing film and again later on *Guns At Batasi* (1964). Regimental Sergeant Major Lauderdale has been hailed as Attenborough's finest performance. Whether that is true or not, he certainly received his first British Academy award for Best Actor.

35

Invitation To The Dance

Hollywood icon, Gene Kelly was producing as well as performing in the aptly named: *Invitation To The Dance* (1955). This lavish musical was partially filmed in London and was to prove a pivotal experience in Roy Ashton's career.

Charles Parker kindly asked me to assist him in the make-up department. It was a very large production I think anyone who was available worked on this picture at one time at least for a day or two. I remember Gene Kelly was under enormous pressure. He sat in the make-up chair one morning surrounded by irate studio executives. They were badgering him for several things at once and wouldn't give him a minute's peace. It was an awful cacophony. Finally, Gene Kelly yelled above the squabbling crowd, "Gentlemen, do you think you could cut it down to a Roar?"

Working on the set of *Invitation To The Dance* Roy met fellow make-up artist Phil Leakey and they soon became firm friends. "I got on splendidly with him, Phil's such a nice bloke" said Roy. According to Elizabeth Ashton "Roy worked as Phil's assistant on many pictures. At this stage of his career he would frequently help other people out but rarely be in charge of make-up." It was Phil Leakey who introduced Roy to a small English production company called Hammer Films. Roy Ashton's life would never be the same again.

Above:
Phil Leakey and
Roy Ashton in a rare
photo together

Roy Ashton:
The Heart of Hammer

(Roy) Ashton's room is the heart of Hammer. He sits here like a benevolent Nanny, surrounded by macabre models, detailed sketches and the surprisingly innocent tools of his grisly trade. Grimacing masks hang from the walls... He displayed his creations with the craftsman's confident pride. "Here is the Mummy coming out of a swamp. Here is a Werewolf. A man with slit ears. Dr Jekyll from the famous story of Dr Jekyll and Mr Hyde. This is something I did for a thing called 'Paranoiac.' One however, a revolting shrunken head has never been used in a film. "I just made that for fun one day, to amuse the company." He said.

The Sub Cinema by Francis Wyndham Sunday Times Magazine March 15 1964

Below:
Phil Leakey and Roy
Ashton: the men who
made monsters.
Far below:
Noses and scars made
from latex...!

In our companion volume *Somebody Mentioned Horror* it is explained how Phil Leakey set up the Make-up Department in 1947, and

HAMMER FILM PRODUCTIONS LTD
JAMES CARRERAS · ANTHONY HINDS · BRIAN LAWRENCE
HAMMER HOUSE · 113/117 WARDOUR STREET · LONDON · W 1
TELEPHONE: GERRARD 9787 *(10 Lines)* - CABLES: HAMMAFILMS LONDON W 1 - TELEGRAMS: HAMMAFILMS, WESDO, LONDON

developed his ground breaking techniques for Exclusive/ Hammer Films. Leakey's expertise became highly regarded by producer, Anthony Hinds. This was because with a handful of other talented artists and technicians, Leakey was able to deliver a first class product, overcoming time and time again, the problems caused by meagre production schedules, lack of facilities, and minuscule budgets. In return, Hinds rewarded Leakey with a highly unusual contract for the film industry at that time. Leakey was retained by the company on a regular salary. This did not prevent Leakey from accepting other film work, such as *Cat Girl* (1957). The idea was that whenever Phil was needed at Bray Studios, he would have to drop other work and return to the fold to work his magic. It was Phil Leakey who supplied Exclusive Pictures with special make-up effects for the

company's science fiction productions, *The Quatermass Experiment* and *X-The Unknown*. By the late 50s, it was decided to make a move towards reviving a more traditional type of fantasy film. The Gothic Horrors, *The Curse of Frankenstein* and *Dracula* propelled Peter Cushing, Christopher Lee and Hammer Film Productions into international reknown.

The Resurrection Of Hammer Films

Hammer Productions Limited began life in November 1934. The production company was the brainchild of Music Hall comedian William Hinds and took its name from his stage persona of 'William Hammer'. Spanish entrepeneur, Enrique Carreras, had set up a distribution company called Exclusive Films Limited. Will Hinds joined the company in 1935, effectively linking Hammer and Exclusive as sister companies. Although ambitious in nature, Hammer only managed to produce a handful of feature films and short subjects between 1935-37. Exclusive Films survived by securing the rights to reissue more lavish and dependable products from London Films and British Lion. Following the Second World War, Enrique's son Lieutenant James Carreras MBE, and his grandson Michael along with Will Hind's son Anthony, began revitalising Exclusive. Under the management of this new generation, Exclusive pursued a vigorous film production strategy and licensed the rights to make screen versions of already popular BBC radio series. In 1949, Hammer Film Productions Limited was incorporated as Exclusive's film production arm. While James Carreras' business contacts attracted American co-production finance, Tony Hinds and Michael Carreras oversaw the actual production operation. They alternated as producers and executive producers on low-budget comedies, war films, musicals and thrillers, eventually concentrating almost completely on the Horror film genre. Exclusive/Hammer preferred to make movies in large private houses rather than incur the overheads of using conventional studio facilities. There were four "house studios".

The first was Dial Close at Maidenhead. It was followed by Oakley Court near the village of Bray then Gilston Park, a country club in Harlow. The final move was to nearby Down Place on the banks of the River Thames. Down Place was eventually remodelled and renamed as Bray Studios.

Bray STUDIOS

"We did these films in those days very much by shooting in the dark. They have enormous appeal to this day. They are still being shown every single day somewhere in the world. Undoubtedly, in proportion to what they cost, they have made more money than any other films in history. It is a fact that the critics didn't really want to discuss very much. It wasn't quite the sort of thing they thought that British films should be known for. But it is true. We kept the industry going with a built-in guaranteed distribution by every American major. When you made a Hammer movie they were all fighting for it.

We used to have a lot of fun in those days, behind the camera, and even in front of the camera, when we knew they weren't really ready to shoot. We had the best food in England. Mrs Thompson - the incomparable 'Mrs T' - used to see to that! The cast and crew kept each other in good temper and it really

Left:
Roy lends a hand or two!

was a happy family. I know that's a cliché, but it really was. It was a little compact studio with a group of people all of whom knew each other very well. I got to the point where I knew what they expected me to do and I predictably did it. Sometimes I surprised them, or tried to. I knew what they wanted and how long we had, whether it had to be take 1, 2 or 3 because we couldn't go any further. It really was a very happy time for me in my career. Probably the happiest I ever had over that period of 15 years. We had our differences of opinion, Hammer and I. They were very tight with money and sometimes they were very obstinate and wouldn't listen to actors or crew. Very often one would work for a director who didn't know how to tell you what he wanted and would rely on you to tell him how to proceed. It happened a lot. I tell you, if it hadn't been for a certain group of people, and I mean the actors and crew, it's impossible to say how those films would have turned out. The major difference, between the films that have been made in this genre in the last 20-25 years, and with us, is this: With us you relied upon performance and story to a tremendous extent. Today, you have special effects on the one hand, make-up on the other. Where is the actor? Somewhere in between? They are just trying to keep their heads above water until the end credits. The Hammer make-ups were really a collaboration between the make-up artist and the performer which had to have the approval of the producer. It was a collaboration and not a confrontation as it is so often these days.

At Hammer, I was working with two masters of their craft. Phil Leakey and Roy Ashton were both artists in everything they did. They had enormous patience and a terrific sense of humour. Both of them saw the funny side and that was a terrifically important factor when one is suffering at the hands of the other."

My working for Hammer happened by accident, really. I had a colleague called Phil Leakey. He was the chap who really introduced me to Hammer Film Productions. I must say that I have the greatest admiration for Phil's work and for his kindness to his colleagues. He would help anyone with the benefit of his experience and wisdom. The false arms which appeared in numerous pictures were made from casting my own limbs in plaster. So I can at least claim to have 'a hand or two' in some of Phil's early work at Hammer Films. Of course Phil designed the make-up for Christopher Lee as the creature in *The Curse Of Frankenstein*, the first of Hammer's Frankenstein films and I was extremely honoured to assist him. This doesn't necessarily imply that the man whom you assist does the whole thing. Sometimes these make-ups are

Roy's sketches for a selection of Victorian characters.

two-man jobs: you might stick a nose on a performer, while the other chap is getting the eyes or a beard ready.

Francis Matthews

"When we worked together on *The Revenge Of Frankenstein*, Roy and Phil used to look through the pages of The Financial Times every morning. Phil's great turn-on was seeing how their shares had done the day before. It was good fun sharing their excitement. Incidentally, Phil was the first person to urge me to buy stocks and shares. I only did it once and it was such a disaster that I never did it again."

Phil Leakey decided to leave Bray Studios in 1958. An associate producer at Hammer, Anthony Nelson Keys, had discovered that Phil Leakey was on a retainer. Intending to save the studio what amounted to a relatively small amount of money, Keys arranged for Leakey's retainer to be revoked. Leakey was furious. Hammer called upon Leakey again to do the make-up on *The Hound of the Baskervilles*. Phil declined, as he was working on another film. "But you are Hammer's make-up chief!" exclaimed the surprised Tony Keys. "Not any more", Phil reminded Keys. "You saw to that!". Hammer and Leakey never worked together again. For the next eight years it was Roy Ashton who supplied the make-up effects for Hammer Films. He expertly utilised the traditional techniques he had learned at British Gaumont before the war. Beards were made, and period make-ups applied. However, Roy was called upon to do more than most make-up artists: he had to design monsters! Little did he know then, that he would create some of the most memorable screen monsters of all time, and be given the title, The King of Horror!.

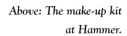
Above: The make-up kit at Hammer.

After Phil Leakey left I was practically non-stop working at Hammer, with about six or seven pictures a year. I was presented with a script but the management only ever had a vague idea of what they really wanted. So I used to make drawings and then sculpt models, so that at least they would get a clearer idea of what they didn't want. Sometimes I would be working on two separate pictures at the same time: The one being shot, and the one I hoped to be employed on next. When that happened I would have about 50 or 60 working drawings on the boil. In this way, I gradually narrowed down the field until they said "Oh yes! That's it go ahead and do that. Many of my best ideas were never used.

Above: Freddie Francis at Hammer.

Freddie Francis (Hammer director and two-time Oscar winner for Cinematography):

"Hammer owed an awful lot to Roy Ashton. He was the perfect guy for them. Hammer were a wonderful business organisation, but I don't think they were ever interested in making films. Really, they were so efficient, they could have been making anything they wanted. They would say to Jimmy Sangster, "Write a script". Jimmy would write the script in no-time, and they would come to somebody like me and say: "Get directing it!". And in about two weeks, we were off and away. So we didn't have the endless round table discussions like planning big movies today. It was rather annoying to go in as the director of a picture, and find that all the sets, and even the make-up designs, had been okayed before you were hired. Then I realised that Hammer worked on this basis. On their schedules and budgets, there was no time to change these things. Roy understood what Hammer were after. He understood what he thought was good and off he went and did it. He was very easy to work with, I don't think that I've ever queried anything that Roy did."

No better crew was ever assembled than that excellent team at Bray Studios. There was a marvellous atmosphere in the studio and although we all worked very hard it was enjoyable. No-one at Bray was ever jealous of anyone else's position. If I had an idea that may have been of use to the property department, for example, it was all welcome. Everyone was invited to contribute to improve the success of a picture. I got on very well with everyone there, particularly Anthony Nelson Keys. He was the studio manager.

It was Anthony Nelson Keys who telephoned Roy when Phil Leakey turned down *The Hound of the Baskervilles*. Keys asked Roy if he would take over the make-up department for that production. Roy was puzzled as to why Phil Leakey was not doing the film, so he told Keys that he would get back to him. A telephone call to Leakey followed, in which Phil explained his dissatisfaction with Hammer. Roy did not wish to invade Leakey's territory, but Phil encouraged Roy to take on the job. With his conscience clear, Roy phoned Tony Keys back, and accepted the position. This was Roy's opportunity to make an impression on Carreras and Hinds.

Above: Milton Reid (The Mulatto) as the "Man with Split Ears" plus Roy's three stage design.

The Hound Of The Baskervilles

Makeup by ROY ASHTON —

Roy's make-up still for Peter Cushing's scar in The Hound of the Baskervilles.

The Hound Of The Baskervilles (1959) was the first time I was in charge of the Make-up department at Bray Studios. The Holmes stories are great favourites of mine. Working on this film brought back so many childhood memories. As a youth, I used to borrow hard bound copies of The Strand Magazine from a librarian friend of my father's in Perth. I spent hours browsing through them copying the Sydney Paget illustrations. I thought Paget's drawings of Sherlock Holmes bore a strong resemblance to the British actor Arthur Wontner. I had the great pleasure of encountering Wontner in Hyde Park one day when I was out for a stroll. This was in the early 1930s, not long after I first arrived in England. Indeed at this time Wontner was widely regarded as the definitive film interpretation of the Master Detective on both sides of the Atlantic. He was even attributed with the legend of routing a party of criminals through his innocent presence in the smoke room of a London pub. Now that's what I call method acting! Later in my career I was fortunate to work on *The Private Life of Sherlock Holmes* (1970) with Christopher Lee who bears the distinction of having played both Sherlock and his brother Mycroft. Of course for many people, myself included, Peter Cushing's interpretation remains the most intriguing Sherlock Holmes. *The Hound Of The Baskervilles* was, I believe, Peter's first performance of the role, but not his last. He informs me that he played the Baker Street Sleuth another 17 times on television, his most recent outing being in the Television Feature Film *The Masks Of Death* (1984) directed by my old friend Roy Ward Baker. I had the pleasure of performing the make-up chores on that film. It is a curious coincidence that I first remember working with Roy on the Gainsborough Picture *Tudor Rose*. This was also the first occasion that I met John Mills. So I felt the circle was completed when Johnny played a stalwart Dr. Watson in *The Masks Of Death*. I didn't have a great deal to do as far as the actor's were concerned on *The Hound Of The Baskervilles*. I think I only had to make a moustache for André Morell. I can't even confirm whether Peter Cushing wore a toupee in the picture or not. It is true he had enough hair in his earlier days. The 'major' problem was suitably equipping the hound with the right appearance. I trust you will forgive my pun when you learn that the Great Dane chosen for the role answered to the name of Major.

Sir Arthur Conan Doyle (1859-1930) first described Sherlock Holme's infamous canine nemesis in the pages of The Strand Magazine April (1902):

"A hound it was, an enormous coal black hound, but not such a hound as mortal eyes have ever seen. Fire burst from its open mouth, its eyes glowed with a smouldering glare, its muzzle and hackles and dewlap were outlined in flickering flame. Never in the delirious dream of a distorted brain could anything more savage, more appalling, more hellish be conceived than that dark form and savage face which broke upon us out of the wall of fog."

Paget's classic illustration of the Hound.

Originally I was asked by the management to see what I could do for the doggy actor. At first, Major behaved himself like an old pro, he was of course held fast by his handler as I applied a one piece, prefabricated mask to his head. The hairy mask fitted like a racing hood allowing Major's ears to protrude and all of the necessary senses to function. I felt that with a little adjustment the mask achieved the desired effect of turning the features of this large but affectionate pet into a ferocious and supernatural killer. However, Major had other ideas. At the first opportunity he innocently licked his lips and dragged his huge paws up from around his ears, down along his muzzle. In one easy movement he removed my handiwork and proceeded to eat it.

Christopher Lee argued: "The make-up on the hound was a failure. We got a Great Dane and tried to make it look very big. The results were very unconvincing!".

Peter Cushing writes in his autobiography, Past Forgetting:

"Eventually, one (dog) was chosen and given a good coating of glycerine. The production team endeavouring to create an illusion of the dog's massive proportions, hit upon the idea of employing three young boys corresponding in relative size to André Morell (Dr Watson), Christopher Lee (Sir Henry), and myself, dressing them in replicas of our clothes. A miniature set was erected depicting a stretch of Dartmoor, clouds of dry ice pumped in, representing fog. The decision was to take a long-shot of this set-up, and when all this was ready for the cameras to turn, a prop man flung a meaty morsel into the set, whereas 'Fido', who'd been starved up until the last moment, pounced upon it ravenously. On the following day the rushes were viewed and disappointment deflated all concerned. We saw three small boys dressed up as if playing a game of charades, foggy toy scenery with a wet, hungry dog in the middle, contentedly wolfing a bone. The sequence was scrapped."

The Hound was a real worry. After lots of suggestions had been discarded, fluorescent grease paint was used and to my delight Major became a special effects job. In *Captain Clegg*, Hammer would eventually adopt a process which was substantially more successful outlining the edges of the

skeletal characters: had they had the Hound done in a similar way, with just the snout gleaming, that would have been much more effective... In the long run the animal hardly appeared in the finished picture at all!

Rosemary Burrows was to work on most of the classic Hammer films with Roy Ashton as an assistant to Molly Arbuthnot in the Wardrobe Department. Rosemary believes that the policy of making do and mending what was available at Bray was at the heart of Hammer's success. She insists that it was light hearted but dedicated team spirit which motivated on all levels of the organisation and made things possible.

*We had a lot of laughs in making these pictures"
Roy Ashton.*

Rosemary Burrows (Wardrobe Department):

"Without that liaison between the Colonel (James Carreras) and Monty (Berman) and the Variety Club (of Great Britain) and that whole thing that went on, we would never have got what we got on the screen. They were really wonderful. Everyone would put up with mending what we had got and making the odd thing we really couldn't afford. I remember running up to the shirt room and saying: 'Could you make me a cravat quickly?' Peter (Cushing) wants to tie it in a special way. And we searched for a piece of fabric or something that would do. It was really "make do and mend" in a way except with Roy and his make-up – it was much more technical."

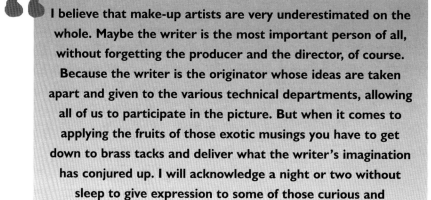

I believe that make-up artists are very underestimated on the whole. Maybe the writer is the most important person of all, without forgetting the producer and the director, of course. Because the writer is the originator whose ideas are taken apart and given to the various technical departments, allowing all of us to participate in the picture. But when it comes to applying the fruits of those exotic musings you have to get down to brass tacks and deliver what the writer's imagination has conjured up. I will acknowledge a night or two without sleep to give expression to some of those curious and impossible situations which they airily described. I don't look back in anger but more in amusement nowadays. I suppose to some degree I was fortunate in my time at Hammer because toiling in 'The Horror Factory' brought me into contact with some of the most charming and accomplished ladies and gentlemen it has been my privilege to work with. To my delight their sense of the ridiculous was almost as great as my own. We had a lot of laughs in making these pictures and there is a continuing air of quality about them. Although they were done on very limited budgets, they were made by a team who really cared about what they were doing.

The Man Who Could Cheat Death

The Man Who Could Cheat Death
Production Details:
Released November 30, 1959
(UK), June, 1959 (US);
83 Minutes; Technicolor;
7488 Feet;
A Hammer Film Production;
A Paramount Release;
Filmed at Bray Studios;
Director: Terence Fisher;
Producer: Anthony Hinds;
Executive Producer:
Michael Carreras;
Associate Producer:
Anthony Nelson-Keys;
Screenplay: Jimmy Sangster,
From Barré Lyndon's Play;
Music: Richard Bennet;
Music Supervisor:
John Hollingsworth;
Director of Photography:
Jack Asher;
Editor: James Needs;
Production Manager: Don
Weeks; Sound Recordist: Jock
May; Camera: Len Harris;
Continuity: Shirley Barnes;
Wardrobe: Molly Arbuthnot;
Hairdresser: Henry Montsash;
Make-Up: Roy Ashton;
Production Design:
Bernard Robinson;
Assistant Director: John
Peverall;
UK Certificate: X.

Cast List:
Anton Diffring (Bonner), Hazel
Court (Janine), Christopher Lee
(Gerard), Arnold Marle (Dr
Weiss), Delphi Lawrence
(Margo), Francis DeWolff
(Legris), Gerda Larsen (Street
Girl), Middleton Woods (Little
Man), Michael Ripper (Morgue
Attendant), Denis Shaw (Tavern
Customer), Ian Hewitson
(Roger), Frederick Rawlings
(Footman), Marie Burke
(Woman), Charles Lloyd Pack
(Man at Exhibit), John Harrison
(Servant), Lockwood West (First
Doctor), Ronald Adam (Second
Doctor), Barry Shawzin (Third
Doctor).

> **The Man Who Could Cheat Death was the first time that I had to make a really complex make-up. That experience put me on the track of many similar subjects.**

The Man Who Could Cheat Death

Jimmy Sangster's screenplay for *The Man Who Could Cheat Death* was adapted from the stage play: *The Man In Half Moon Street* by Barré Lyndon. In the Hammer version the lead role of Dr. Georges Bonner had been designed for Peter Cushing, but he declined the offer. According to Hazel Court: "Peter Cushing said it was all too much for him. He felt he was being offered too many parts that were roughly the same."

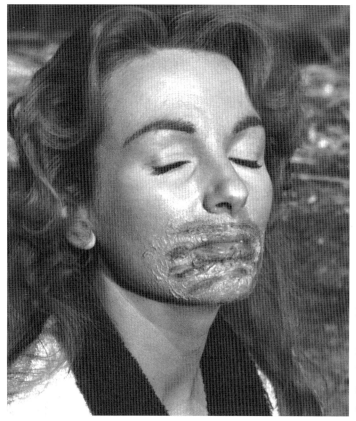

The casting problem was solved when Anton Diffring was signed to replace Peter Cushing for a second time, in the same year. The first provided Diffring's Hammer debut earlier in 1958 as Baron Frankenstein in *The Face In The Tombstone Mirror*, a pilot programme for an aborted TV series, *Tales Of Frankenstein*.

In *The Man Who Could Cheat Death*, research scientists Georges Bonner and Ludwig Weisz discover a way to halt the ageing process. This requires an operation on Bonner to replace his utter-parathyroid gland with a fresh specimen, every ten years, courtesy of a hospital post mortem, or murder. Unprotected from the ravages of time, Weisz suffers an incapacitating stroke and Georges searches for another surgeon. Meanwhile, he avails himself of a life preserving fluid which will allow him to survive for up to four weeks after the allotted time to replace the gland. Unfortunately because the fluid will also temporarily affect his mind, Georges loses all control and unleashes a psychopathic rage against anyone who dares to stand in his way.

"His touch burned the woman's face like vitriol".
Delphi Lawrence (Margo)

Hazel Court

"I thought that Anton Diffring had a 'coolness' that was perfect for the role of Georges Bonner. He was very serious and never displayed a great deal of humour during the making of the film. He always seemed to be thinking of something else when you spoke to him. I could never really get to know him."

Bonner's discarded mistress Margo Philippe (Delphi Lawrence) uncovers the secret of his dependency on the precious fluid. In his splendid novelisation, Jimmy Sangster describes several of the challenges for Roy Ashton's make-up:

Georges turned to face her suddenly. "It's too late," he said. His body was infused with a strange inner light similar in colour to the one trapped in the safe. It had impregnated his bone structure so that the bones showed clearly through their coverings of flesh. He was a living and moving skeleton, the skull gleaming with a green, unearthly light, his hands skeletal spiders. From the grinning skull stared two incredibly bright eyes, shot with the same hellish glow. One of the spiders that were his hands reached out towards Margo. "Too Late" said the skull "too late." Margo's scream of terror was cut off as Georges whipped out his hand and clapped it across her mouth. With his other hand he grabbed her across the shoulders, ripping her dress and allowing her breasts to tumble

free. For a moment they stood close together, the beautiful half naked woman and the ghastly green skeleton that held her. Then Margo's eyes started to dilate with pain and from beneath the skeletal hands a thin wreathe of smoke curled upwards. There was a sizzling sound, a crackling of scorched flesh... Across her face, where his hand had choked off her cry, was a vivid, deep seated, burn scar, of puckered blistered flesh. A similar scar was burned deep into her shoulder and left breast where his other hand had held her powerless. Even now there was a stink of burning flesh in the air, and Georges wrinkled his nose in disgust. He looked at Margo for a long time, then he reached out and touched her burned face gently. "I tried to tell you Margo...I did try."

His touch burned the woman's face like vitriol. I had to pucker the whole lower half of her face and part of the upper arm in the shape of his fingers. A later scene required an effect in which this injury had been clogged with dirt as a result of her forced imprisonment. The effect was livid with suppuration at the centre and was copied from an illustration in a medical text book. I later collected quite a library filling several scrap books. As a rule I always cut-out anything of interest from magazines and periodicals, which I assume may possibly be of use in a future project.

Hazel Court

"I played Jannine Dubois the woman

Above:
Ashton's moustache nestles on Christopher Lee's top lip.

Left:
A detailed schematic of Diffring's final make-up.

Georges Bonner plans to make immortal like himself. Anton Diffring was supposed to be sculpting me so they had to do a full plaster cast of my head and torso. Roy was very gentle. He explained the process and then put a straw in my mouth and covered my head to take a cast. It was very unpleasant and the plaster became quite hot around my

47

The Man Who Could Cheat Death

face. Later, I remember how they took me to the plasterer's shop and wrapped my upper body in gauze. Then they covered me in plaster. I will always remember the plasterer laughing, and saying: 'It's like slapping a wet fish around!' When I am posing for Anton they shoot over my back and shoulder in the finished movie, but we also did a nude torso scene for overseas. They said they would pay me a little extra and I said: 'If it works and it's beautiful then that's fine by me.' The idea of an artist who sought to preserve the beauty of women in stone and clay, because they would be his only lasting companions was very romantic. It was an idea that really appealed to me and I felt that it actually enhanced the film."

After all the trials and tribulations regarding his make-ups in *The Curse of Frankenstein* and *Dracula, The Man Who Could Cheat Death* must have provided welcome respite for Christopher Lee. Co-starring in the role of Dr. Pierre Gerrard,

Above: Ashton uses watercolour to express his desired effect.

Right: "The Man Who Could Cheat Death certainly taxed my ingenuity" – Two early make-up tests.

48

the surgeon blackmailed into performing the vital operation on Bonner, Lee is resplendent in a debonair, moustache hand-woven by Roy.

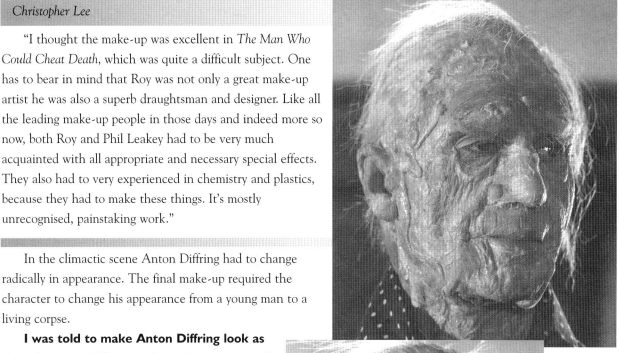

Christopher Lee

"I thought the make-up was excellent in *The Man Who Could Cheat Death*, which was quite a difficult subject. One has to bear in mind that Roy was not only a great make-up artist he was also a superb draughtsman and designer. Like all the leading make-up people in those days and indeed more so now, both Roy and Phil Leakey had to be very much acquainted with all appropriate and necessary special effects. They also had to very experienced in chemistry and plastics, because they had to make these things. It's mostly unrecognised, painstaking work."

In the climactic scene Anton Diffring had to change radically in appearance. The final make-up required the character to change his appearance from a young man to a living corpse.

I was told to make Anton Diffring look as though he was falling to pieces. To produce all the ravages of time and debauchery, I felt that the final effect should be a cocktail of fatal diseases spreading rapidly across his body. Glandular fever, smallpox, cholera, typhus and typhoid, represented some of the ailments that Bonner had come into contact with (through his unseen travels) as a crusading physician. In addition I designed a set of special contact lenses to create the milky white and yellow effect of an old person's eye. A good deal was achieved by stretching his skin and putting liquid rubber onto it. By letting it dry on a pinch of skin and returning to its original position you can fashion all the carbuncles and crinkles you desire. I also prepared things that would go straight on a plastic cap. I used mending wool from an old blue cardigan to imitate collapsing veins. For instance, I pinned a number of threads into the required shape and coated them with latex. When this substance had set, I removed the supporting pins and there was the vascular system I was looking for! The original application process took about four hours. With practice I was able to short cut the more ponderous techniques, chiefly by getting pieces ready beforehand so that I had them at my disposal in the morning. That reduced the application time to approximately two hours. Anton complained bitterly. He said: 'My God! If I had known what all of this involves I would never have accepted the role!'.

Above: "My God! If I had known what all this involves, I would never have accepted the role!" Further make-up tests.

The Man Who Could Cheat Death

"Was I ever intimidated by Phil or Roy's make-up creations? Looking back, I did find the ending frightening on *The Man Who Could Cheat Death*. I thought Anton Diffring was a strange person anyway. So when the make-up did all those things to the poor man's face and body and he became old and diseased, I personally could connect with that effect and couldn't wait to get the scene over and done with!"

Despite the complexity involved in this make-up, it can only be glimpsed in the final moments of the film. However, as an indication of Roy's influence in the story of cinema history, there is a post script. Over a decade later, American make-up artist Dick Smith was working on *Little Big Man* (1970). He was puzzled by how to give Dustin Hoffman the convincing appearance of a 103 year old man. Smith called Phil Leakey in England to ask him how he had accomplished such a realistic effect in *The Man Who Could Cheat Death*. Phil explained that this was Roy Ashton's work, and not his. Happily, Leakey put Smith in touch with Roy Ashton, who forwarded detailed instructions to Smith in Hollywood. Smith has adapted Ashton's work several times, most recently for the Mel Gibson fantasy, *Forever Young* (1992).

Above:
The First Hammer
Scream Queen –
Hazel Court.

Right: Anton Diffring in
Circus of Horrors

The Man Who Could Cheat Death certainly taxed my ingenuity. I worked with Anton Diffring very shortly afterwards on *The Beast Must Die* (1974), then I didn't see him again until about 20 years later, when I did *The Masks of Death*.
I do hope he wasn't avoiding me!

The Mummy

The Mummy:
Released September 25, 1959 (UK), December, 1959 (US); 88 Minutes; Technicolor; 7903 Feet;
A Hammer Film Production;
A Rank Release;
Filmed at Bray Studios;
Director: Terence Fisher;
Producer: Anthony Hinds;
Executive Producer: Michael Carreras;
Associate Producer: Anthony Nelson-Keys;
Screenplay: Jimmy Sangster;
Music: Frank Reizenstein;
Music Supervisor: John Hollingsworth;
Director of Photography: Jack Asher;
Editor: Alfred Cox;
Supervising Editor: James Needs;
Production Manager: Don Weeks;
Sound Recordist: Jock May;
Camera: Len Harris;
Continuity: Marjorie Lavelly;
Costumes: Molly Arbuthnot;
Egyptology Adviser: Andrew Low;
Hairdresser: Henry Montsash;
Make-Up: Roy Ashton;
Masks: Margaret Carter Robinson;
Assistant Art Director: Don Mingaye;
Production Design: Bernard Robinson;
Assistant Director: John Peverall,
Second Assistant: Tom Walls;
Third Assistant: Hugh Harlow;
Focus: Harry Oakes;
Clapper: Alan McDonald;
Boom: Jim Perry;
Sound Camera Operator: Al Thorne;
Sound Maintenance: Charles Bouvet;
Stills: Tom Edwards;
Publicist: Colin Reid;
Casting Director: Dorothy Holloway;
Assistant Casting Director: Chris Barnes;
UK Certificate: X.

Cast List:
Peter Cushing (John Banning), Christopher Lee (Kharis), Yvonne Furneaux (Isabelle/Ananka), Eddie Byrne (Inspector Mulrooney), Felix Aylmer (Stephen Banning), Raymond Huntley (Uncle Joe), George Pastell (Mahemet), Michael Ripper (The Drunken Poacher), John Stuart (Coroner), Harold Goodwin (Pat), Denis Shaw (Mike), Willoughby Gray (Dr Reilly), Stanley Meadows (Attendant), Frank Singuineau (Head Porter), George Woodbridge (Constable), Frank Sieman (Bill), Gerald Lawson (Irish Customer), John Harrison (Priest), James Clarke (Priest), David Browning (Sergeant).

66 **When I first read the script for *The Mummy* I noted the principal requirements needed for make-up. The poor chap was to be mutilated; his tongue cut from his mouth to prevent him from revoking the curse placed upon him; he was to return to life a few thousand years later with the traditional appearance of mummification and then he was to be resurrected from a muddy grave, only to be blown apart in the film's finale. Not very much to ask for I thought!** 99

The Mummy

With their innovative rewordings of *Frankenstein* and *Dracula*, Hammer Films gambled upon repeating the box office business of the old Universal movies and quickly negotiated access to the complete back catalogue of horror film subjects. This was the first time a major Hollywood studio had made such an agreement with a British company. "In the first instance", according to screenwriter Jimmy Sangster, "Hammer was told by Universal to come up with a remake of *The Mummy* and so that was what they got." In actual fact, the Sangster screenplay was not a simple remake of the 1932 film. Instead the narrative blends story elements from the original John L. Balderston screenplay based on a story by Nina Wilcox Putnam and Richard Schayer, with the four other Universal Pictures in the "Mummy" series. A starting point for Roy's make-up design called for detailed research into Egyptology.

I had to find the answers to many questions. How was the body preserved on the long journey across time? Do the bandages completely disintegrate? Do the eyes, nose or ears disappear? In those days there was considerable interest in the subject of Mummies. I made several visits to the British Museum in London where I attended an extensive exhibition of artifacts. I believe some intrepid archaeologists had just discovered another Pharaoh in a remote tomb somewhere. In any event, there was an actual Mummy on display and I was able to make a close examination of the remains. I discovered that the custom of Mummification flourished between 2400 BC and the 4th century AD. The Greek Historian Herodotus left a detailed account of this curious process.

They take first a crooked piece of iron, and with it draw the brain through the nostrils, thus getting rid of a portion, while the skull is cleared of the rest by rinsing with drugs. Next they make a cut along the flank with a sharp Ethiopian stone, and take out the whole contents of the abdomen, which they then cleanse, washing it thoroughly with palm wine, and again frequently with an infusion of pounded aromatics. After this they fill the cavity with the purest bruised myrrh, with cassia, and every sort of spice except frankincense, and sew up the opening. Then the body is placed in natron (hydrated carbonate of sodium) for 70 days and covered entirely over. After the expiration of that space of time, which must not be exceeded, the body is washed, and wrapped round, from head to feet, with bandages of fine linen cloth, smeared over with gum, and in this state is given back to the relations who enclose it in a wooden case which they have made for the purpose, shaped into the figure of a man.

Greek Historian Herodotus

Roy Ashton's records detail several methods of Mummification. One consists of injecting cedar wood by syringe. This dissolved the stomach and intestines, which were drained out through the anus. The body was then soaked in natron, which eradicated the flesh, leaving only skin and bones. Bitumen was also an essential ingredient which was used in packing the cavities from which the organs had been removed. This had the effect of blackening the body, adding to its weight and making it practically indestructible. Roy noted that the word mummy is itself derived from an Arabic term meaning bitumen.

The Mummy was to be the first major collaboration at Hammer between Roy Ashton and Christopher Lee. Roy explained, "When Christopher Lee played the first Frankenstein, I knew little of the pre-production discussions – and only at the finishing stages did I come into contact with him".

The challenge for Roy Ashton was to reinvent what many fans would regard as one of the icons of horror. Could he equal the legacy of his hero, Hollywood make-up legend Jack Pierce, and provide a suitable appearance for any actor wishing to follow in Karloff's sandy footprints?

Once the shooting script is finalised, I take this home and the first conceptions are put into sketch form. Approval and development – sometimes unfortunately rejection – is the next stage. When the basic idea is established I model the idea in miniature in the round – and again if no alterations are suggested a full size model in clay or plasticine is set up. This is photographed by the "stills" man – and the final decisions made. By this time, the original artist, in this case, Christopher Lee, will have been brought

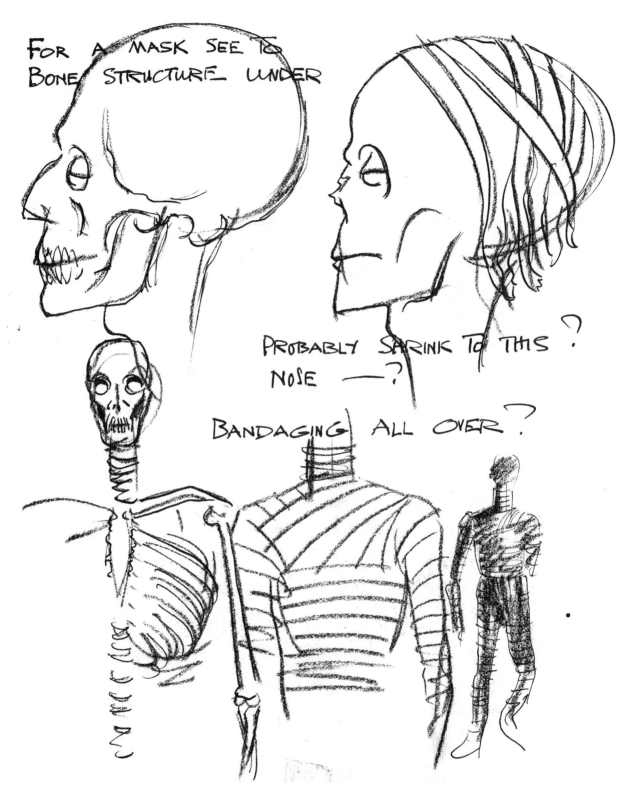

FOR A MASK SEE TO
BONE STRUCTURE UNDER

PROBABLY SHRINK TO THIS ?
NOSE —— ?

BANDAGING ALL OVER ?

to the studio – and a replica of his head in plaster will stand on my modelling table. Upon this I model the changes corresponding to those indicated in my drawings or upon my clay model.

The enthusiastic amateur may lack the means to make a plaster cast reproduction, but can always manufacture a 'head' close to the dimensions needed from wool and work on that! The things you will need are – a lot of old rags and bits of paper, rubber adhesive, and copydex or Bateman's household adhesive. I use Revultex, but any of the latex materials are

Above:
Sketches show the skeletal
framework upon which
Ashton based his Mummy

53

The Mummy

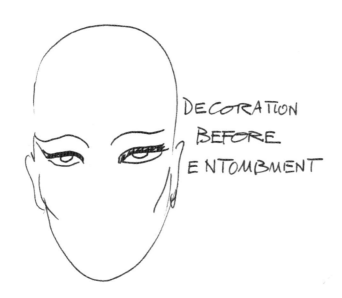

DECORATION BEFORE ENTOMBMENT

excellent. Some Vaseline is needed to smear very lightly on your model's head to act as a separator. If you wish to alter the contours of the Mummy's head, you will need to build up the shape you want in plasticine. Then use strips of old rag joined by latex, gradually winding them to suggest old and rotting bandaging. It's a good idea to start with a zip fastener as I feel it easier to build up to this. Make your strips of bandage by tearing up the old rags Then work away with your rag strips, one over the other, until you have a covering forming a complete mask around the head. Keep sticking them on, roughly following the shape of the neck. Don't worry

FIRST UNCOVERING BANDAGES ROTTING FALLING AWAY

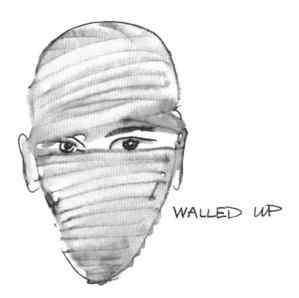

WALLED UP

....

Four stages of mummification

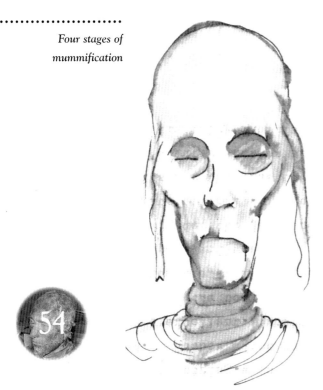

ROTTING

too much about their shape, after all a few millennium underground is going to spoil them a bit. To remove the finished results, simply open the zip when everything is quite dry and lift it off. You then recast this shape, making a female mould, into which you can cast an identical form in plastic or papier mache. The latter material is very light in weight and rests on the artist's head, supporting the outer structure as a mask.

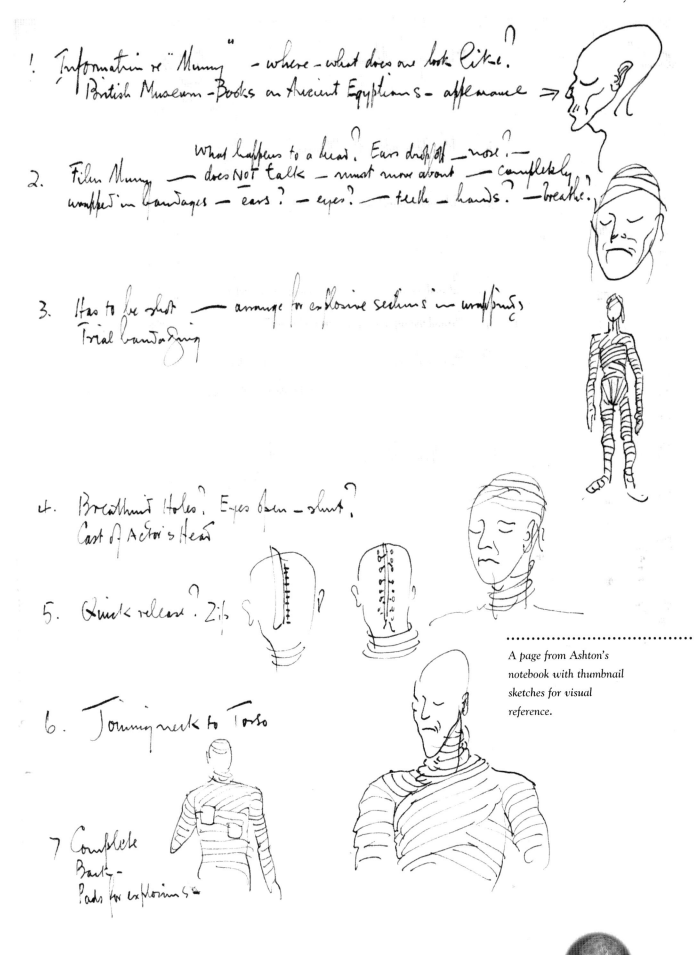

1. Information re "Mummy" — where — what does one look like?
   British Museum — Books on Ancient Egyptians — appearance ⟹

2. Film Mummy — does NOT talk — must move about — completely
   wrapped in bandages — ears? — eyes? — teeth — hands? — breathe?
   What happens to a head? Ears drop off — nose? —

3. Has to be shot — arrange for explosive sections in wrappings
   Trial bandaging

4. Breathing Holes? Eyes open — shut?
   Cast of Actor's Head

5. Quick release? Zip

6. Joining neck to Torso

7. Complete
   Back —
   Pads for explosions

A page from Ashton's
notebook with thumbnail
sketches for visual
reference.

WHAT'S A MUMMY LOOK LIKE?

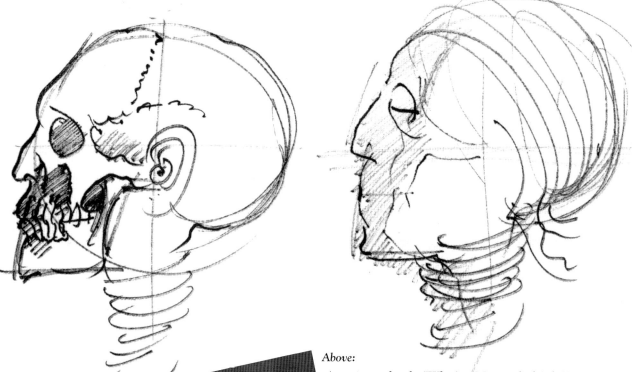

Above:
Attention to detail - "What's a Mummy look Like?"
Left:
Life mask of Christopher Lee used for modelling purposes.

Christopher Lee:

"*The Mummy* – that was a tough one. The make-up was really more in the nature of a mask like putting on a pilot's flying helmet. It fitted tight over my head and Roy pulled the zip down the back which got it flush to my skull."

I had to apply the final windings fabricated from worn out rags one by one until the whole head was clothed. Then with rubber and plastic skin I shaped the face. This operation would take about one hour and a half. When we were busy on Christopher's face he needed something to write on, to communicate with, as he wasn't able to talk. Christopher was an excellent performer to work with, a most co-operative gentleman. Unfortunately, I didn't realise that the mummy mask would adhere so close to his face. Also there was nowhere for him to breathe. There were no holes underneath the nose area. It didn't occur to me that anything under the nostrils on the mask would scarcely be visible anyway. I'm afraid he had to inhale through his eye holes which was very uncomfortable for him.

Ashton examines the performance of his creation. How could he improve the mechanics of the design?

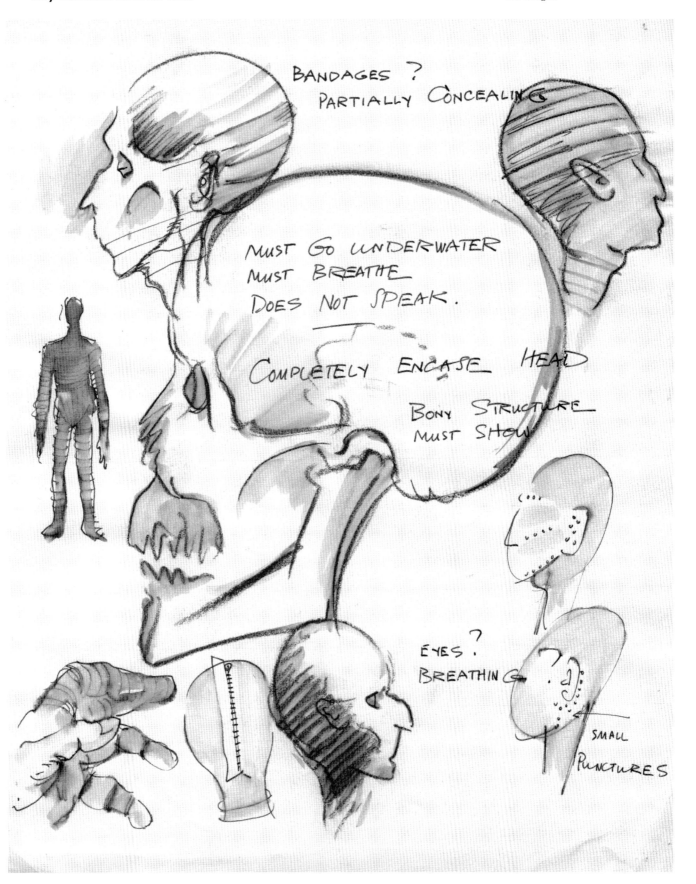

58

Roy collaborated with Hammer wardrobe mistress Molly Arbuthnot in creating the Mummy costume.

The coverings for the trunk arms and legs were a matter of patient winding and sewing. I made detailed notes and drawings of how the funeral bindings had been applied to actual Mummies. But I must admit we learned more from modern day medical procedures than ancient Egyptian sorcerers.

Christopher Lee remembered: "It was very difficult wearing those bandages, I couldn't get out of them once they were on me. It would take too long to get out and get back in." Roy and Molly managed to reduce the many hours involved in applying the wrappings and ageing techniques by producing what Roy called a 'Mummy tunic with a zipper on the back.' Christopher Lee pointed out that: "You can see from the photographs that a swathe of bandages had to be contrived to go around my shoulder and all the way around my back to cover up the zip."

Christopher Lee:

"My whole body had to convey the idea to the audience that *The Mummy* was an unstoppable automaton. The walk like a robot – the stride: I worked that out myself. In many ways Kharis is very human in his reactions, especially when he meets the reincarnation of his beloved Princess. The only way I could show this was with my eyes. I suggested a certain sadness, a certain shame and longing with an angle of my head. I relied upon mime to suggest; "Oh No! this is my great love reincarnated and here am I and what a terrible mockery of the exalted human being I once was."

Christopher is such an expressive actor that instead of hating the

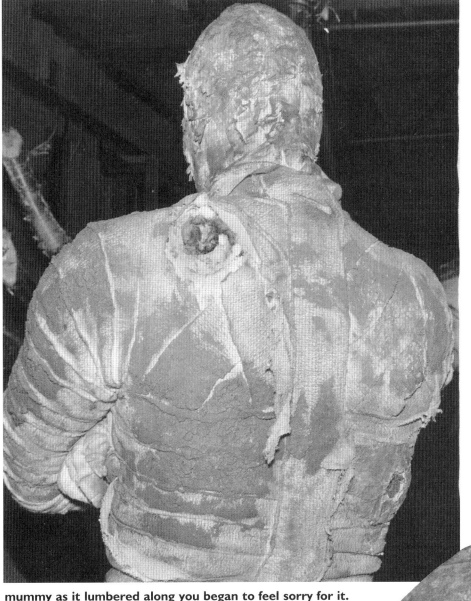

This page and opposite
show various views of the
test make-up

**mummy as it lumbered along you began to feel sorry for it.
This is the thing with all these poor creatures in the early
Hammer Films, I don't think anybody really dislikes them.
Beneath the grotesque exterior each one struggles with a
very humanising dilemma. That's why I have never felt
ashamed of the genre in which I work.**

Christopher Lee:

"With the Mummy mask on, I could say what I liked,
because my real mouth was unseen. This of course gave us a lot
of laughs in the making of that film. The swamp I had to wade
through was filled with pipes and all sorts of underwater gear
which caused the mud to bubble. It was quite funny because the
face of the mummy was without expression, and here am I
"F"ing and blinding away at the top of my voice about
these awful metal pipes crashing against my
knee caps underneath the mud. On
each take I would stride out into the

tank bang my knees and release this stream of rude words at the top of my voice, all from behind a totally immobile and absolutely rigid, face. Everyone laughed themselves silly! I always tried to create humorous moments, often doing anything to make it bearable, actually. I remember in an earlier scene on that picture, Peter (Cushing) was stood beside me. There was a gap in the conversation and I leaned towards him and said in a high pitched voice: 'I'm just waiting for someone to say: "Just don't stand there - kill someone!" Then I can go home to the wife and kids!' Peter thought that was one of the funniest things he had ever heard."

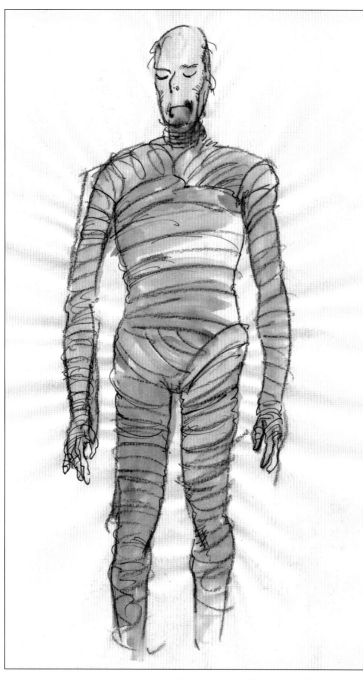

A full length sketch.

At Hammer, artists frequently had to spend several hours per day in the make-up chair. We would start very early in the morning, when there was almost no-one else in the studio. During these marathon sessions I would try to get them off to sleep, but some people preferred to sit and chat. This could even be an occasion for a great deal of fun, especially with Christopher Lee. He has such a great interest in music and an encyclopaedic knowledge of opera. He and I would invariably begin to sing in friendly rivalry, intercut by hideous laughter. An aria from the many works known to us both would be commenced by one of us and left for the other to finish.

Christopher Lee:

"Roy and I used to sing all the time. I'm a bass baritone and of course, he was a tenor. Whilst working on *The Mummy* we would flit from opera to opera in the morning just to keep ourselves going."

We had a loudspeaker system at the studio, and if you pressed a certain number on the switchboard, you broadcast all over the place! So, the most awful sounds could be heard first thing in the morning. I suppose if any passers-by might have heard us they could have thought we were quite mad! Peter Cushing had such a marvellous sense of humour that when he heard our versions of some of the celebrated duets, we had to refrain from singing another note in case he injured himself!

During each Hammer production Roy had to make at least two completely different sets of identical character make-ups; one for the actor playing the creature and duplicates for the artist's stunt double.

"Most actors wouldn't want someone else to wear their gear anyway. But then again most of my make-up doesn't survive the scene. Actually, it was Roy Ashton who suggested that I double Christopher Lee in the first place. I was working on a film called *The Death of Uncle George*. At the time I didn't know who the hell Christopher Lee was!"

"Christopher was always in very good shape" recalls Eddie "and he likes to do his own stunts whenever he can." Eddie revealed it was Christopher Lee who smashes through the French windows in *The Mummy* to reach Peter Cushing and launch one of the most memorable fight sequences in the Hammer canon. The origin of this sequence relies in part on Peter Cushing's innate professionalism and his feeling that Hammer should never intentionally mislead the audience. Having seen the film's presale publicity Cushing was genuinely troubled by the image of the Mummy with a gaping hole in its torso. The image was made more striking because the beam of light from a constable's Bull's eye lantern penetrates the hole in the Mummy's back, emerging from his stomach to illuminate his face.

It was a wonderfully imaginative way to convey the physicality of *The Mummy* as a hollow entity which cannot be destroyed. However, searching through the script Cushing could find no action to account for the injury. The idea of the poster promising something that wasn't in the film was intolerable to him. On Cushing's insistence a fight sequence was developed in which his character plunges a harpoon through the Mummy's stomach and resorts to firearms in an effort to destroy his supernatural foe.

A ghostly vision...

"emerging from swamp".

In practical terms that meant building in stronger parts in the upper torso with a metal backing. This precaution was to protect Eddie Powell from any chance injury from the special effects appliance.

"I had two small explosive charges on my chest and I had to trigger them off myself. Peter Cushing blasted me once with the shot gun and fired again with the other barrel. It worked very well and these two monster holes appeared in my suit. Terence Fisher was extremely pleased. However, when I was cut from the bandages I discovered I was covered in black powder. That stuff gets right into the pores of your skin. I had a devil of a time getting it out and had to soak in a bath before I could start thinking about making my way home."

Roy was asked to reprise his mummy make-up six years later for *The Curse Of The Mummy's Tomb*. However, Christopher Lee was probably relieved to be replaced in the role of the Mummy by Dickie Owen. Roy did make a number of improvements to the original prototype. He devised a make-up which allowed for the freer circulation of air and included a series of concealed apertures through which perspiration could escape. Roy also contrived various cavities in the Mummy make-up to relieve unnecessary pressure on the actor's face and body.

I had to work on the Mummy's make-up. After his first screen test Dickie Owen's face mask was thought to need strengthening. So, I modelled much bigger temples and cheeks but followed much the same procedure as in the Chris Lee version. The artist's eyes must be able to negotiate his surroundings. In the original design Chris Lee's eyelids were painted black and were visible through slits in the face mask. This was sufficient to allow him to see but prevented convincing close-ups of the Mummy's eyes. In the subsequent Mummy picture I made mummified 'eye covers' resting on the artist's eye lids, and as they moved naturally with the artist's own eyes he could see perfectly.

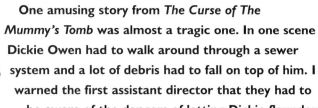

A miniature model of a Mummy sculpted by Roy Ashton.

One amusing story from *The Curse of The Mummy's Tomb* was almost a tragic one. In one scene Dickie Owen had to walk around through a sewer system and a lot of debris had to fall on top of him. I warned the first assistant director that they had to be aware of the dangers of letting Dickie flounder around in fairly deep water. "Don't worry Roy. It'll be all right!" I was told. However as Dickie tried to make his way through that destruction, he failed to keep his balance, lost his footing and got water all over him. He dipped beneath the surface and had to fight for his breath. Well I had a feeling that something like this might happen and I was standing by with a pair of scissors. I leapt in and speedily cut him free, helping him to discharge the water from his throat. One cannot be too careful about those situations.

As a result of this potentially fatal mishap, Owen was replaced in this scene by Eddie Powell.

Eddie Powell:

"I was carrying this bird and the scroll of life through the sewer and at a certain point I had to go down and hold myself under the water. The rig I was wearing was a bastard to get under water. They thought it would take two days to shoot. I did it in one take. Michael Carreras said I'd saved them a lot of time and money and they would double what I was getting in the contract. Hammer was a marvellous company to work for."

In two or three additional takes in *The Mummy* and *The Curse of the Mummy's Tomb*, we piled on cuts, broken legs, etc. a little more. These

scenes were supposed to depict the cruelty of certain Egyptian ceremonies. I was given to understand that scenes such as these were more permissible in certain foreign markets.

In retrospect, unlike Pierce's wonderful creation, which was glimpsed only in the opening minutes of Universal's film, Roy's interpretation of a living mummy dominated Hammer's most lavish production to date. The notion of immortality and the burden this invariably comes to represent for reanimated beings, and in the case of the mummy – an unfortunate creature who is not allowed to die – echoed the themes previously developed in *The Man Who Could Cheat Death*. These themes haunted Roy's future work and resulted in at least two more masterpieces of fantasy cinema make-up: *She* and *The Plague of the Zombies*. Roy's ideas of life, death and immortality assumed great importance in his life – both personally and in his films, and provided a deep and enduring source of inspiration.

Beneath the superficial appearance of the human face there are etched many depths of experience. They reflect glimpses of birth, life and death that fuel the perpetual queries of the artist and the philosopher. These experiences, which go to fashion a person's character and motivation in life, and dare I say the afterlife, are very private. Indeed they are sacred.

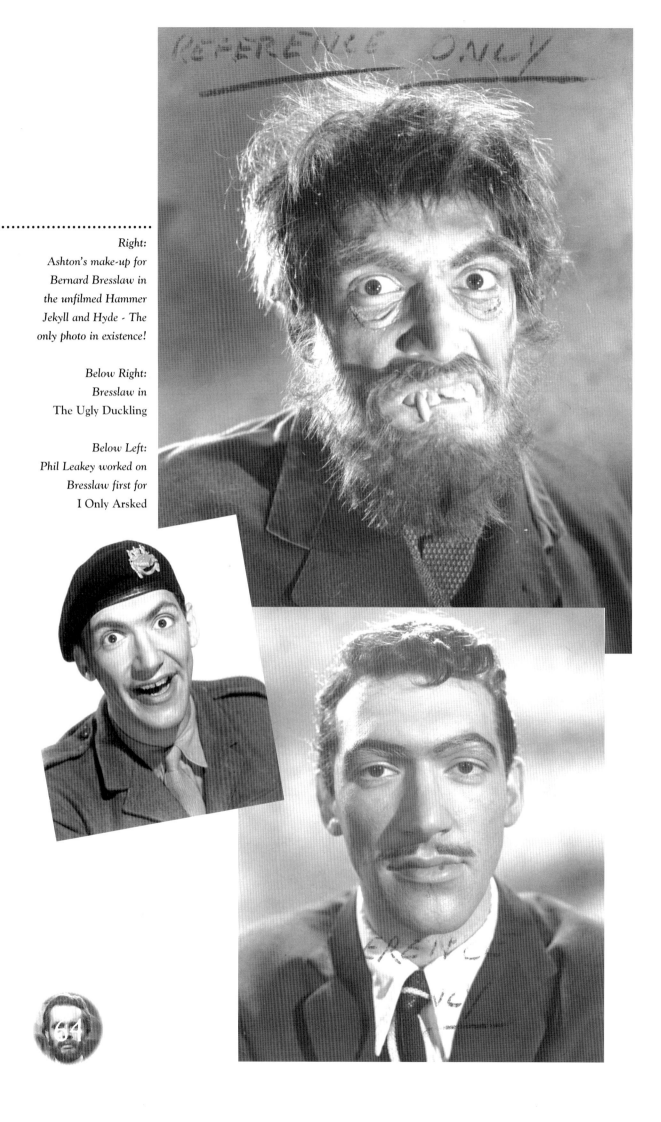

Right:
Ashton's make-up for
Bernard Bresslaw in
the unfilmed Hammer
Jekyll and Hyde - The
only photo in existence!

Below Right:
Bresslaw in
The Ugly Duckling

Below Left:
Phil Leakey worked on
Bresslaw first for
I Only Arsked

64

The Two Faces Of Dr. Jekyll

The Two Faces Of Dr. Jekyll Production Details: Released October 24, 1960 (UK), May 3, 1961 (US); 88 Minutes; Technicolor; Megascope; 7878 Feet; A Hammer Film Production; A Columbia (UK) American International (US) Release Filmed at Bray and Elstree Studios; Director: Terence Fisher; Producer: Michael Carreras; Associate Producer: Anthony Nelson-Keys; Screenplay: Wolf Mankowitz, Based on Robert Louis Stevenson's Novelette 'The Strange Case of Dr Jekyll and Mr Hyde'; Music and Songs: Monty Norman and David Hencker; Music Supervisor: John Hollingsworth; Director of Photography: Jack Asher; Editor: Eric Boyd-Perkins; Supervising Editor: James Needs; Production Manager: Clifford Parkes; Sound Recordist: Jock May; Camera: Len Harris; Continuity: Tilley Day; Costume Designer: Mayo; Wardrobe: Molly Arbuthnot; Dances: Julie Mendez; Hairdresser: Ivy Emmerton; Make-Up: Roy Ashton; Assistant Art Director: Don Mingaye; Production Design: Bernard Robinson; Masks: Margaret Robinson; Assistant Directors: John Peverall; Second Assistant: Hugh Marlow; Sound Editor: Archie Ludski; UK Certificate: X.

Cast List: Paul Massie (Jekyll/Hyde), Dawn Addams (Kitty), Christopher Lee (Paul Allen), David Kossoff (Litauer), Francis DeWolff (Inspector), Norma Marla (Maria), Joy Webster, Magda Miller (Sphinx Girls), Oliver Reed (Young Tough), William Kendall, (Club Man), Pauline Shepherd (Girl in Gin Shop), Helen Goss (Nanny), Denis Shaw (Hanger-on), Felix Felton (Gambler), Janine Fay (Jane), Percy Cartwright (Coroner), Joe Robinson (Corinthian), Joan Tyrill (Major Domo), Douglas Robinson (Boxer), Donald Tandy (Plain Clothes Man), Frank Atkinson (Groom), Arthur Lovegrove (Cabby).

...Is it the mere radiance of a foul soul that thus transpires through, and transfigures, its clay content?

Robert Louis Stevenson

The Two Faces of Dr. Jekyll

Hammer had made a previous attempt at the Jekyll/Hyde story with *The Ugly Duckling* (1959). Roy had designed the make-up for this comic spoof starring Bernard Bresslaw, who plays a moronic descendant of the original Doctor Jekyll. Hammer introduced an original twist into the Robert Louis Stevenson story by having Bresslaw rediscover his ancestor's mystic potion and change himself into debonair gang leader, Teddy Hyde. The concept was further developed in Jerry Lewis' *The Nutty Professor* (1963). Oddly, Hammer intended to produce two Jekyll and Hyde films with Bernard Bresslaw – one a comedy, and one a serious interpretation of the Stevenson novel. Michael Carreras commented in Kinematograph Weekly (28 May 1959) that "the two treatments are so far apart as to be practically unrecognisable. *The Ugly Duckling* will do the straight version some good. It will reacquaint people with the names Jekyll and Hyde." The film

Three make-up test stills of Paul Massie

was unenthusiastically received, and the idea of continuing with the serious version with Bresslaw was scrapped. One may wonder what the evil Hyde, played by Bresslaw, might have looked like. Roy Ashton had designed a make-up for Bresslaw for use in the Hammer Jekyll and Hyde which was never made. For the first time ever, we are publishing Roy's own photograph of Bresslaw in that make-up.

Although deciding not to proceed with the serious Bresslaw version, Hammer did not wholly abandon the idea of a serious treatment of this subject. Of course, Dr. Jekyll and Mr. Hyde had already been filmed numerous times, including classic versions starring Fredric March (1931) and Spencer Tracy (1941) in the title roles. Because of this long track record, Hammer engaged screenwriter Wolf Mankowitz to come up with yet another new angle. Instead of becoming a repulsive monster, a rather morose,

Chart to indicate progressive changes in MAKE-UP for MR. Paul MASSIE

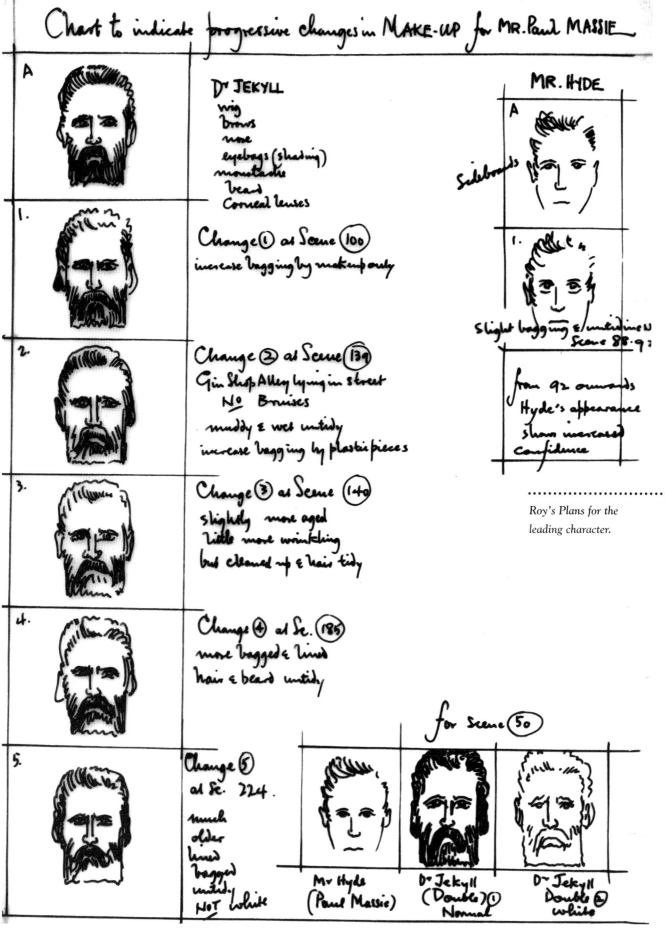

A

Dr JEKYLL
wig
brows
nose
eyebags (shading)
moustache
beard
Corneal lenses

MR. HYDE

A

Sideboards

1.

Change ① at Scene ⑩⓪
increase bagging by makeup only

1.

Slight bagging & untidiness
Scene 88.9?

2.

Change ② at Scene ⑬⑨
Gin Shop Alley lying in street
N̲O̲ Bruises
muddy & wet untidy
increase bagging by plastic pieces

from 92 onwards
Hyde's appearance
shows increased
Confidence

....

Roy's Plans for the
leading character.

3.

Change ③ at Scene ⑭⓪
slightly more aged
little more wrinkling
but cleaned up & hair tidy

4.

Change ④ at Sc. ⑱⑤
more bagged & lined
hair & beard untidy

for Scene ⑤⓪

5.

Change ⑤
at Sc. 224.
much
older
lined
bagged
untidy
NOT White

Mr Hyde
(Paul Massie)

Dr Jekyll
(Double)①
Normal

Dr Jekyll
Double②
white

67

*Two preliminary sketches
of the make-up for
Paul Massie*

bearded Jekyll sheds twenty years to become a charming, clean-shaven seducer Edward Hyde. The twist in Mankowitz' script resulted in Canadian actor, Paul Massie being put in the unusual position of playing the monster without any disguising make-up while he wore a more substantial make-up to play Dr. Jekyll. This character make-up may have seemed substantial, at least to the viewer, but rather routine for Roy.

That was a very light make-up, in fact. However, did you know Paul Massie had a false nose on? I didn't want to do it quite as it finally appeared, yet that was what Michael Carreras wanted at the time. It worried me as I put it on. I didn't like it. And then, when I saw it on the screen I couldn't stand it at all!

Once again, Roy Ashton was disappointed at not being challenged by one of the screen's greatest make-ups. He had greatly admired the Fredric March make-up in particular, and sincerely wanted to do an "Ashton" Hyde.

'There is something wrong with his appearance; something displeasing, something downright detestable... God bless me, the man seemed hardly human! Something Troglodytic, shall we say?

Robert Louis Stevenson in The Strange Case of Dr. Jekyll and Mr. Hyde (1886)

We can get some idea of what he might have done by examining his drawing for Stage No. 5. This was conceived before Mankowitz' script was finalised, and shows how the Hyde character would have appeared. Roy had planned a brilliant transformation sequence, only to be informed by the Studio that it would not be required. All we have is a tantalising glimpse from the "sweepings of the make-up room floor", as to what might have been. As it turns out, it is the Jekyll character here who is to be hideous. The make-up is subtle and suggestive, no doubt disappointing Hammer fans, hoping to see another classic Ashton monster. Nevertheless, it is easy to dismiss the less spectacular make-ups as facile, when this is far from the truth. Clearly, Roy made it look easy. However, examine his work for the make-up on Paul Massie. From the earliest sketches, through a detailed character sheet, to a wonderfully innovative use of tracing paper over a test still, Roy Ashton proves that he could deliver whatever his taskmasters at Hammer required.

Left:
A rare glimpse of Ashton's conception of the original Hyde character... Stage No.5!

Below:
An innovative use of tracing onto vellum in planning Jekyll's appearance.

> **Screenwriter Wolf Mankowitz said; "Evil is attractive to all men. Therefore is it not logical that the face of evil should be attractive."**

The Vampire Make-ups

Dracula
Production Details: Released June 16, 1958 (UK), May 8, 1958 (US); 82 Minutes; Technicolor; 7332 Feet; A Hammer Film Production; A Rank Release (UK), Universal International (US) ; Filmed at Bray Studios; Director: Terence Fisher; Producer: Anthony Hinds; Executive Producer: Michael Carreras; Associate Producer: Anthony Nelson-Keys; Screenplay: Jimmy Sangster based on Bram Stoker's novel; Music:James Bernard ; Music Supervisor: John Hollingsworth ; Director of Photography: Jack Asher ; Editor: James Needs; Production Manager: Don Weeks ; Sound Recordist: Jock May; Camera: Len Harris; Continuity: Doreen Dearnaley; Wardrobe: Molly Arbuthnot; Hairdresser: Henry Montash; Make-Up: Phil Leakey (Assisted by): Roy Ashton; Production Design: Bernard Robinson; Assistant Director: Robert Lynn; Special Effects: Syd Pearson; UK Certificate: X.

Cast List: Peter Cushing (Van Helsing), Christopher Lee (Count Dracula), Michael Gough (Arthur Holmwood), Melissa Stribling (Mina Holmwood), Carol Marsh (Lucy Holmwood), John Van Eyssen (Jonathan Harker), Olga Dickie (Gerda), Valerie Gaunt (Vampire Woman), Geoffrey Bayldon (Porter)

   I don't think it was ever our intention to make Dracula into a hideous monster. The vampire exists beyond the pleasure and pain of life, and is denied the natural release of death.

Roy Ashton worked on the first four vampire movies produced by Hammer Films: *Dracula* (1958), *Brides Of Dracula* (1960), *Kiss Of The Vampire* (1962), and *Dracula, Prince of Darkness* (1966). During his time at Bray Studios, Roy played a vital role in Hammer's Gothic revision of the un-dead. The tone and structure of these movies established the ground rules for future film vampires and vampire hunters alike. However, in the late 50s this successful formula was yet to be developed. Working in collaboration with Phil Leakey, Roy faced a daunting challenge when Hammer Films finally received the go-ahead from Universal Pictures to remake *Dracula*. As Phil Leakey announced: "Familiarity breeds contempt and the problem with the character of Dracula at that time revolved around creating a credible appearance for a vampire. There is a thin line between generating dramatic tension and laughter".

Unlike the previous Universal films, Hammer's *Dracula* was appropriately set in the late Victorian age. The already unsettling plot was laced with ground-breaking special make-up effects in graphic Technicolor, and the results were startling. There was another key reason for Hammer's success, according to director Terence Fisher. "The whole basis of the story of the first Dracula wasn't particularly Dracula himself. It was the effect that he had upon his victims, particularly his female victims". For the first time on screen, Dracula had a powerful sexual identity: one that epitomised the seductive concept of evil. If Hammer can be said to have returned Dracula to his rightful place, leading the way for a new host of cinematic vampires, then it was Phil Leakey and Roy Ashton who drained the pallor from his skin, crafted the splendid fangs, and filled his eyes with blood red lust. The image of Christopher Lee as Dracula was to be forever associated with the names of Leakey and Ashton.

Dracula

I remember it was a very foggy day when Phil Leakey gave me a call to go along to Bray Studios to help him out for two or three days with the make-up on *Dracula*. When I arrived at the studios I couldn't find anywhere to park. After cruising around the grounds of this large country house I found what I thought was a deserted graveyard. I decided to park up my car. And as soon as I had done this Phil came running towards me. 'My Gawd!' said Phil. 'You can't leave your car there, that's the set!' Fortunately there was no harm done and everyone had a good chuckle about it.

In Jimmy Sangster's screenplay, Jonathan Harker (John Van Eyssen) is no longer the innocent abroad. He travels to Castle Dracula with the expressed intention of ending 'this man's reign of terror'. Within the dungeons Harker stumbles across the sleeping body of a beautiful vampire (Valerie Gaunt). After having a wooden stake driven through her heart she reverts to her real age – changing into a hideous old woman. Sangster's words inspired a startling transformation on screen, but the scene proved remarkably difficult to capture on film.

Geoffrey Bayldon:

"Roy Ashton had reason to remember our first meeting. I was a sprightly young man when I walked into the Make-up room at Bray. Roy said: 'Good morning, can I help you?' And I said: 'Yes my name is Geoffrey Bayldon.' He said 'What are you playing?' I said 'The old hall porter.' He said: 'God Almighty! We'll have to start on it straight away.' He began work on my hair crimping and whitening it. Halfway through the assistant director came in and spoke into Roy's ear with hushed excitement: 'By the way', he said, 'whisper, whisper, downstairs, whisper, whisper, whisper'. They had a little conference and Roy said: 'I'm sorry Geoffrey. Would you mind getting out of the chair. There's someone needed on the set before you.' In came a little old lady, who was put into the make-up chair. In the next half hour or so she turned from a sweet little old lady into an old lady looking like a piece of Gorgonzola cheese. This all happened 'before my very eyes!' as stage magicians used to say. When Roy had finished work on the old lady, she was taken back downstairs to the set. I got back into the chair and Roy began the crimping and the ageing work again. Then there was a terrible commotion and the news filtered up that there was trouble on the set."

Phil Leakey explained that no-one had told the old lady that she was expected to remove her dentures, and climb into a sarcophagus. "This lady flatly refused to take out her false teeth. It was very cold that day. Eventually I managed to entice her to play along and even climb into this stone coffin. But it took several large brandies" remembered Phil. "Then she got a bit sozzled and proceeded to demolish the rest of the bottle."

Peter Cushing (from his autobiography, Past Forgetting):

"The shot called for a close-up of her face as she lay in a deep lidless coffin. That was all the old darling had to do - just lie there, no dialogue, no action. The scene took some time to set up and light, and just when everything was in apple-pie order, ready for shooting, a break for lunch was called and we all trooped off to the canteen. An hour later, when we reassembled, the double was missing. A frantic search ensued but to no avail. Terence Fisher, the director, had just decided to get on with another scene to save wasting any more precious time, when a gentle snore came from the interior of the casket. There she was, cosy and warm under the huge arc lamps, an angelic smile on her face, having nodded off before lunch, and remained there ever since. Terry gently roused her, and with the sweetest imaginable smile she looked up into his eyes and said drowsily, 'I'm quite ready when you are Mr Fisher.'"

Bram Stoker (Dracula 1887):
"Then there was the sound of rattling chains and the clanking of massive bolts drawn back. A key was turned with the loud grating noise of long disuse, and the great door swung back. Within stood a tall old man, clean shaven save for a long white moustache, and clad in black from head to foot, without a single speck of colour about him anywhere."

Phil and I decided to ignore Stoker's description of the character as we wanted to create a younger more virile image for Dracula. I understand that this was the first time in film history that Dracula wore fangs. It was my responsibility to fit Christopher Lee's vampire fangs and remove them after shooting.

The size of the fangs are often exaggerated in posters and books. In actual fact they are not much bigger than Christopher's own teeth and slide

Brides Of Dracula
Production Details: Released (UK) August 29, 1960, September, 1960 (US); 85 Minutes; Technicolor; 7674 Feet; A Hammer - Hotspur Production; A Rank Release (UK), Universal International (US); Filmed at Bray Studios; Director: Terence Fisher; Producer: Anthony Hinds; Executive Producer: Michael Carreras; Associate Producer: Anthony Nelson-Keys; Screen Play: Jimmy Sangster, Peter Bryan, and Edward Percy; Music: Malcolm Williamson ; Music Supervisor: John Hollingsworth; Director of Photography: Jack Asher; Editor: James Needs and Alfred Cox ; Sound Recordist: Jock May ; Camera: Len Harris; Continuity: Tilly Day; Wardrobe: Molly Arbuthnot; Hairdresser: Frieda Steiger; Make-Up: Roy Ashton; Art Director: Thomas Goswell ; Production Design: Bernard Robinson; Assistant Director: John Peverall; Special Effects: Syd Pearson; UK Certificate: X.

Cast List: Peter Cushing (Van Helsing), Martita Hunt (Baroness Meinster), Yvonne Monlaur (Marianne), Freda Jackson (Greta), David Peel (Baron Meinster), Miles Malleson (Dr. Tobler), Michael Ripper (Driver), Andree Melly (Gina)

quite easily over his canines. I applied a light colouring all over his face with highlights on the cheek bones. Vampires are supposed to be excessively hairy

so I joined his eyebrows together through subtle shading, to suggest a wilder, more ferocious side to his nature, even when he pretends to be normal. His hair is raven black in colouring and brought to a slight triangular point over the forehead in a kind of widows peak.

In those days there were no special allocations of money to produce special effects make-ups. We had to do them with just our ordinary facilities and it was very taxing indeed. Phil Leakey and I had great difficulty in coping with what was required sometimes. It forced us to cultivate our own resources, mostly at home on the kitchen table. For the final sequence showing Dracula decomposing into a pile of dust Phil and I had to work closely together with the special effects unit under the supervision of Syd Pearson. It was a highly complicated process. Phil had manufactured pieces of treated paper to fix around Christopher's face, and little sacks filled with powder. Christopher Lee had to scrape his hand over them to dislodge small reservoirs of blood, dislodging and releasing the powdered skin. I had to restore them from time to time, as they ran empty when several takes had to be made. This was just maintenance, of course, as Dracula's face had to be made up for each progressive stage of decomposition. The special effects people would handle the dissolves between one make-up job and the next. But as to who does what in a sequence varies from picture to picture. For example, when I was in charge of make-up at Bray I usually handled the scenes which involved abrasions and flowing blood – such as when a vampire was impaled on a stake or when Dracula opened up a cut on his chest for a lady victim to drink from – but these days the special effects men usually do all that. If during a pre-production meeting, the effects man says 'I will do all the scenes involving blood' I don't argue with him because it will save me a lot of bother.

Above:
Christopher Lee as the definitive Dracula, designed by Phil Leakey

Dracula's disintegration: "A highly complicated process"

Brides Of Dracula

Jimmy Sangster

"The first draft of Brides was written as 'Disciple of Dracula'. I had been told to write a sequel to *Dracula* by Tony Hinds, but he specified: "Lets not go overboard on Chris Lee.""

Christopher Lee was replaced in the lead role by David Peel. Baron Meinster was another vampire aristocrat who corrupts the students of a girls school.

David Peel was excellent in the part of Baron Meinster. I thought his reaction to being burned by holy water was very good. The effect was based on medical illustrations of unfortunate people scalded by hot fat. This required the manufacture of several rubber pieces. Unfortunately David left the industry after the picture was completed and returned to the stage. Martita Hunt played his mother, the wicked old Baroness. She had great fun in the scene where she hides her fangs from Peter Cushing in a coquettish fashion behind a lace veil. I think on the whole, *The Brides of Dracula* is rather unfairly overshadowed by the first *Dracula*. I think its still quite effective in a spine tingling way. Years later, I was travelling in France and I wanted something to read before going to sleep. So I picked up a film magazine (Midi-Minuit Fantastique No.1, May - June, 1962) which contained an article on the psychological significance of blood as used in Hammer Film Productions. I thought that was very strange, because all I did was pick up the telephone and say: 'I want half a dozen bottles of Technicolor No. 2'. or something to that effect. I don't see much psychological significance in that! I didn't realise I was so good...

In Christopher Lee's absence, Peter Cushing's Van Helsing takes centre stage in *The Brides of Dracula*.

Roy wrote about his high regard for Peter Cushing in an article for *The Cushing Companion*:

It has been my pleasure to have known Mr. Peter Cushing for many years and to have assisted him in my capacity as make-up artist on many film productions. Sometimes a make-up artist will anticipate the arrival of a star name with some anxiety, for occasionally their temperaments may be unpredictable. This has never been the case with Mr. Cushing. I have always looked forward to lend a hand as well as I can. Mr. Cushing always forms a

Kiss Of The Vampire Production Details: Released September 11, 1963 (US), January 6, 1964 (UK); 88 Minutes; Eastmancolor; A Hammer Film Production; A Rank Release (UK), Universal Release (US); Filmed at Bray Studios and Black Park; Director: Don Sharp; Producer: Anthony Hinds; Screen Play: John Elder, ; Music: James Bernard; Music Supervisor: John Hollingsworth; Director of Photography: Alan Hume; Editor: James Needs; Sound Recordist: Ken Rawkins; Camera: Moray Grant ; Continuity: Pauline Wise ; Wardrobe: Molly Arbuthnot ; Hairdresser: Frieda Steiger ; Make-Up: Roy Ashton; Art Director: Don Mingaye ; Production Design: Bernard Robinson; Assistant Director: Douglas Hermes; Special Effects: Les Bowie ; UK Certificate: X.
Cast List: Clifford Evans (Professor Zimmer), Noel Willman (Dr. Ravna), Edward de Souza (Gerald Harcourt), Jennifer Daniel (Marianne Harcourt), Barry Warren (Karl Ravna), Jacquie Wallace (Sabena Ravna), Isobel Black (Tania), Peter Madden (Bruno), Vera Cook (Anna)

Two bottles of blood used by Roy Ashton

75

The Vampire Make-ups

*Peter Cushing by
Roy Ashton*

*The definitive
Vampire Hunter*

very accurate picture of the character he is to represent. He is most meticulous in the process of building up that role. His scripts have detailed notes, descriptions of costume, the progress of the plot. Many a continuity secretary would do well to examine his scripts as splendid examples of detailed study. The costume department has to look well to its successive plot detail, for Mr. Cushing will certainly be well aware of every change – of every progressive movement down to the finest detail. The make-up artist has to watch carefully the appearance of his artists throughout the shooting of the film, and so I watched Mr. Cushing almost times without number. During all the years I have watched I have never even seen him hesitate over his lines. He is invariably word perfect. What an example for some of our players! If they could match his splendidly prepared characters, and most efficiently conducted artistry, the problems for producers would be much diminished. Every aspect of Mr. Cushing's art is quality – and again quality – and that also applies to his personal disposition. Supporting artists along with all members of the crew are treated to the same consideration shown to his fellow stars. Mr. Cushing's courtesy and kindness to fellow artists are a delight. No outbursts are seen. I sometimes drew caricatures of Mr. Cushing in his various roles and they were a source of great amusement to him.

(Some of the caricatures of Peter Cushing can be seen in the Prologue of this book.)

Peter Cushing (personal correspondence with Roy Ashton):

"I was deeply touched to read your wonderful tribute in 'The Cushing Companion'. Thank you so very much, dear fellow. I am not ashamed to say it made me blub! What a wonderful fellow you are!"

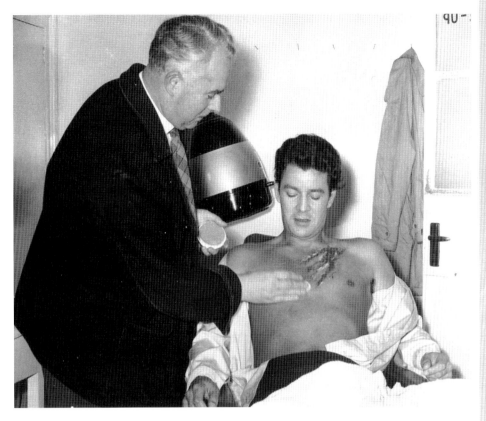

Dracula, Prince of Darkness
Production Details: Released
January 9, 1966 (UK), January
12, 1966 (US); 90 Minutes;
Technicolor (UK); 8100 Feet; A
Hammer Film Production; A
Warner - Pathe Release (UK),
20th Century Fox (US); Filmed
at Bray Studios; Director:
Terence Fisher; Producer:
Anthony Nelson Keys;
Executive Producer: Anthony
Hinds; Screenplay: John
Sansom (Jimmy Sangster), based
on an idea by John Elder (Tony
Hinds) based on the character
created by Bram Stoker; Music:
James Bernard; Music
Supervisor: Philip Martell;
Director of Photography:
Michael Reed; Supervising
Editor: James Needs; Editor:
Chris Barnes; Production
Manager: Ross Mackenzie;
Sound Recordist: Ken Rawkins;
Camera: Cece Cooney ;
Continuity: Lorna Selwyn ;
Wardrobe: Rosemary Burrows ;
Hairdresser: Frieda Steiger ;
Make-Up: Roy Ashton; Art
Director: Don Mingaye;
Production Design: Bernard
Robinson; Assistant Director:
Bert Batt; Special Effects: Les
Bowie; UK Certificate: X.

Cast List: Christopher Lee
(Dracula), Barbara Shelley
(Helen), Andrew Keir (Father
Shandor), Francis Matthews
(Charles), Suzan Farmer
(Diana), Charles Tingwell
(Alan), Thorley Walters
(Ludwig), Philip Latham
(Klove)

Kiss Of The Vampire

With the original working title of 'Dracula III', *Kiss Of The Vampire* reached the screen without either Christopher Lee or Peter Cushing. This film featured a chateau full of bloodsuckers who prey upon an unwitting couple on their honeymoon in Bavaria. Professor Zimmer replaced Van Helsing as the resident vampire expert. As in *Brides of Dracula*, the hunter becomes the hunted and must free himself from the curse of vampirism.

Tony Hinds always thought that we could take these things one step further. In *Kiss Of The Vampire* instead of using a red-hot poker to reverse the effects of the vampire's bite, as Peter Cushing had done previously, the character of Dr. Zimmer actually plunges his hand into a purifying flame. The effect was achieved by making a cast of Clifford Evan's hand and soaking it in inflammable liquid. I was also instructed to make the vampire fangs far longer than in the original production.

The Harcourts are invited to a masked ball at Chateau Ravna. This was conceived as an opulent affair in the screenplay, a visual means to explore the themes of

Top of page: Roy creates the effect of a vampire clawing Edward de Souza's chest
Above: Roy's masks on display at the Vampire Ball

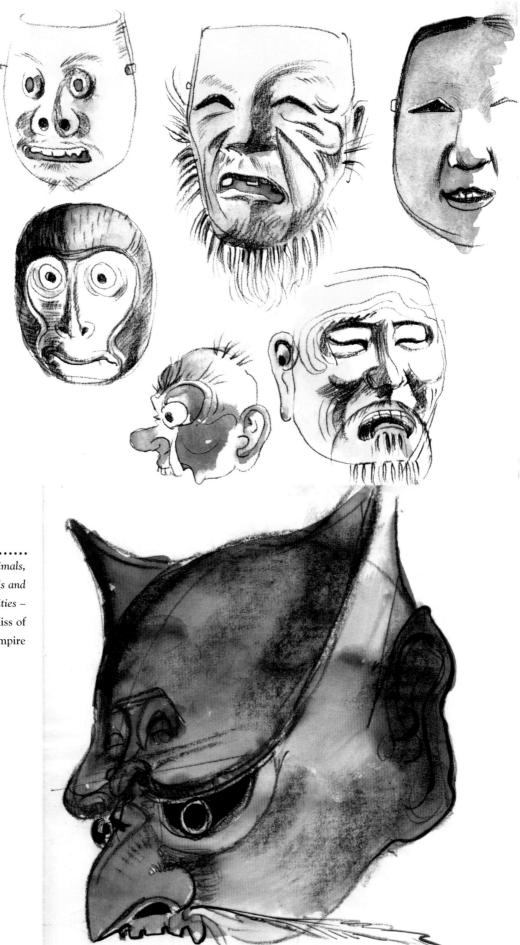

Birds, animals,
Devils and
monstrosities –
masks for Kiss of
the Vampire

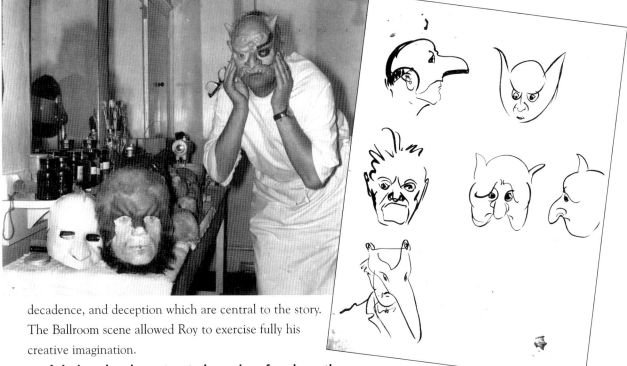

decadence, and deception which are central to the story. The Ballroom scene allowed Roy to exercise fully his creative imagination.

I designed and constructed a series of perhaps three dozen masks for the ballroom sequence. This was great fun as I developed all sorts of fantastic creations for the artists to wear. These included birds and animals, devils and monstrosities.

One mask, in particular, was to become one of Roy's personal favourites. A horned face with a beak-like appearance had another smaller face superimposed upon it. This mask design was always included in the sketches Roy did for his own amusement.

Top left:
Roy tries on his favourite
mask. Note werewolf
appliance in foreground

Below:
Roy demonstrates how to
apply a vampire bite.

Dracula, Prince of Darkness

Jimmy Sangster:

"Peter Cushing was a lovely guy and we got on very well but he never really thought very highly of my writing. When Christopher Lee was thinking of doing *Dracula, Prince of Darkness*, he told me he had called Peter on the phone. He said to Peter: 'I've just been offered a Jimmy Sangster script and there's no dialogue for my character'. 'Congratulations old boy!' Peter said."

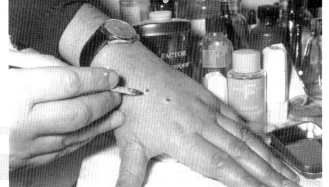

Christopher Lee:

"I have always made it plain I didn't want to play Dracula again. There was a gap of eight years and I didn't speak in the second one at all. That was because I read the script and I just wouldn't say any of the lines, because they were verging on the absurd. I have never held it back, we did a lot for each other, Hammer and I, and they still used to argue on every film about salary. 'We can't afford you now. You must make this film and we can't afford you'. When I turned them down I would

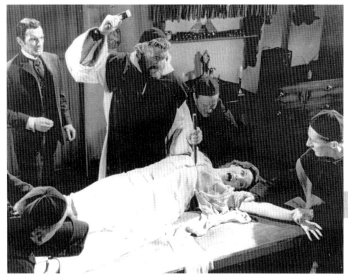

The staking scene in
Dracula, Prince of
Darkness

get telephone calls from James Carreras pleading with me, saying: 'I'm begging you. I'm too old for all this worry. I'm begging you to make these films because if you don't, think of the people you will put out of work: the technicians, the actors and actresses.' This was a terrible thing to do to an actor. If he wanted to approach me he should have done so through my agent. He should never have done that to me personally. It was a terrible thing to do. He would 'phone me and say: 'We will give you a piece of the action.' Of course it was a piece of the producers nett. And of course I used to give in, but I didn't want to do those films."

Francis Matthews.

"In spite of the fact that Hammer had built up a very big international reputation they were still operating in a very small family way. I think *Dracula, Prince of Darkness* was one of the top money makers in America that year. When we were making it, there were quite a lot of producers and directors and all the money people dropping in from America. I think they were studying the method of shooting and how Hammer could make them so quickly for so little money. The Americans were interested in how they could do the same and retain the same quality. There was a slightly more high powered atmosphere around by then. Tony Hinds was a little more distant. He had been very pally on *The Revenge Of Frankenstein* but he seemed to have a lot more cares on his shoulders by the time we did the second Dracula. Tony Nelson Keys was just the same, he was lovely. Roy and I used to bump into each other occasionally outside Bray. In our profession you pick up relationships as though you had never been apart. It's very strange. You can be away for years from someone, and you start work together again and almost immediately you pick up where you left off. There's no transition period of getting to know each other again, its like you worked with them the day before, and years can have passed. Back then I had a rather arched surprised look because of my eyebrows and Roy taught me how to soften them, with very fine pencil painting. It worked very well and I've used it ever since when I do my own make-up in theatre. Working in films or on television, you can't really explain to other make-up people what your favourite make-up man has done for you. So I go to my dressing room and adjust it myself. Roy was very charming and gentle and fun and he didn't try to show off with his make-up. Some make-up artists that I've worked with have been fairly self assertive in so far as they have regarded themselves as more important than the actor in a way. But Roy was never like that, he was unobtrusive and yet highly efficient. He never, never got upset about anything that happened. He was always cool and calm and everybody was very fond of him."

Barbara Shelley

"The make-up room was always referred to as 'Roy's Room'. We went to have a talk with Roy and have our make-ups put on. He was a very even-tempered man. I always found I had to be very wide awake in the mornings or I would start to go to sleep under the make-up. It was nice to have a very professional relationship with a make-up man because you could say "Look Roy, that's a bit swollen on this side can you fix it?"

Dracula, Prince of Darkness provided Barbara Shelley with one of her most memorable roles for Hammer. In the film, she is transformed from a shrewish housewife into a sexual tigress by Dracula's 'kiss'.

Barbara Shelley

"All of us took the classical approach to our work. I asked myself: 'What is a vampire? It's evil!', so I said: 'Okay, it's like one of the Greek Furies' and took it from there. I believe horror films are all about the hidden side of everyone's humanity. For instance: Why do vampires want to bite a virgin's neck? I think it's because you want someone to bite yours. There was this elderly lady who I once met. She was a grandmother and she told me that she liked horror films, which amazed me. She said 'Oh, but I don't like the ones that they do now. I don't like them at all!' She was rather adamant so I asked her why she felt like that and she said: 'Too much sex and not enough neckbiting.' She had never equated neck biting with sex in any way. It was a completely innocent view of being frightened and about having your neck bitten. It was wonderful."

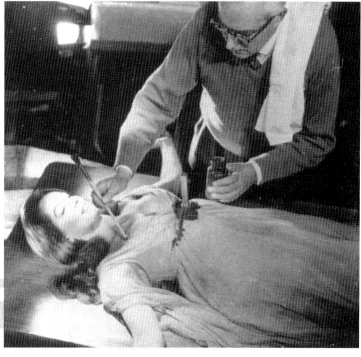

Francis Matthews:

"We had a lot of laughs working on *Dracula, Prince of Darkness*. It was all fairly ridiculous. When you were in the middle of doing it, you did feel a bit of a fool. During filming, I had to come rushing into a room and find a man with red eyes and a huge cloak and large teeth and my sister-in-law in her night-gown with equally large teeth, trying to bite my wife's neck. And all I said was "Let her go." It was fairly understated dialogue. They always either over wrote it, or under wrote it. In that situation what you would probably do is faint, or say: 'What the hell is going on?' But instead of that I said: 'Let her go' and dashed across the room."

Roy puts the finishing touch on to Barbara Shelley.

Barbara Shelley:

"I had the scene coming up where I had to walk down the stairs towards Suzan Farmer. I knew I had to talk with my fangs in. The line wasn't up to much but I was happy, because Michael Reed was doing the lighting and it took a long while to get it right, so I could practice what I had to say. I came down the stairs and walked towards the camera and said: 'Snarl, gwaft ptalle plaanking fluur loosch Dlannasch!' 'What on Earth was that?' some one said from behind the camera. They shouted: 'Don't you mean: We have been waiting for you Diana?' I took out the false teeth and said: 'That's what I said, but these fangs are sticking in my mouth.' They said: 'Okay we'll dub it in later.' I said: 'No you bloody won't!' I think it was the only line that I had to say in that scene and I got it in the end. But it was very difficult to talk with those fangs in your mouth. Chris never spoke you see. He was laughing to himself out of shot. So I said to him: 'Clever so-and-so!' And he laughed all the more! The staking sequence caused the biggest problem for me with the fangs. I was spread-eagled on a table top, held down by several large monks. Andrew Keir drove a large wooden stake through my chest. After Terry Fisher had done the master shot he said: 'That was okay, but

Below:
Roy's tin of Vampire Bites: "Now ventilated to let wounds breathe"

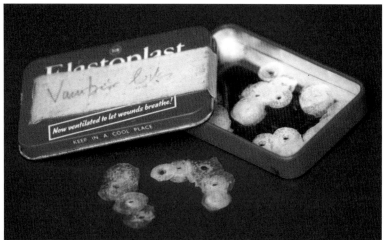

Barbara's face was turned away from me for most of the scene. It spoiled the effect, we'll have to do it again!' 'Terry' I said: 'The reason my head was turned away was that I've swallowed a fang and I was trying to hide it!' Terry's face was completely blank but his shoulders were moving up and down. He always did that when he thought something was funny and was trying to hold back the laughter. 'Never mind darling', he said: 'We'll do it again in a couple of days, when the other fang shows up.' 'If it ever does show up', I replied, 'I won't be putting that thing back in my mouth.'

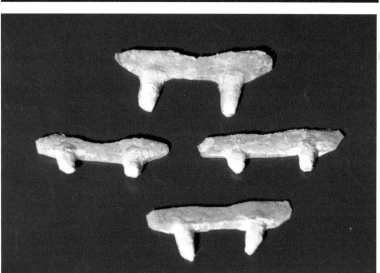

Above:
Latex vampire teeth for long shots.

When making a set of vampire teeth you first need an impression of the dental structure of the artist involved. This I think is a process most people would know about, but for those who don't: You take a tiny tray which will overlap the teeth, fill it with a moulding substance, press this over the teeth, wait about five minutes and then you have a female mould of the dental structure, or gums if the artist is toothless. Into this mould you pour dental plaster and wait for it to harden. This will give you a replica of the inside of the artist's mouth. Dental technician's might smile to read such a simplified account. In short you model whatever changes you wish to make in dental wax and make fresh casts of these, reproducing your modelled teeth in acrylic. I must point out that making dental appliances are best left to dental professionals while the design of the plate should be arrived at in consultation with the make-up artist. I used to make all my fangs myself, but I don't do that any more because a dental technician has got all the necessary facilities at his disposal and is so accustomed to doing these things that he can knock them out in a tenth of the time that I

can. The usual way of producing vampire fangs is as jacket crowns. These fit over the actor's real teeth like caps. But a dental technician makes them for me with a little plate so there's none of the bother of worrying whether they are going to stick on or not: they just clamp in behind the tooth and the normal canines just rest on this denture he makes. Dental materials are freely available and can be used for many purposes other than fang making. For instance you can make excellent skulls and other bones.

Christopher Lee

"The most uncomfortable make-up to wear are the contact lenses which were hell for me and gave that red effect that people still ask about. You really can't see very well if your not used to it, because they have to cover the whole eye and everything went blurred. I couldn't keep them in for more than 15 minutes, I would start to cry. They are dreadful if you are not used to them."

With Chris Lee I would put the contact lenses in just before filming started and remove them immediately afterwards. This was so he wouldn't be distressed by them. Some people just can't develop a tolerance for contact lenses, particularly if they suffer from hay fever. The ones that Christopher wear cover the whole of the eye except for the cornea and iris and fit under the upper and lower lids.

Francis Matthews:

"On one occasion, Roy dropped a contact lens on the floor. The set was supposed to be covered in snow, but it wasn't real. It was actually salt. Roy cleaned the contact lens but he obviously hadn't got every single speck of salt out of it. He put it in Christopher's eye and then he had a terrible time of it. He had to go away and have his eyes washed out. I don't think it was a great drama but it was obviously very painful for him."

I think what made those vampire pictures different was, although we had an awful lot of fun behind the camera, the themes were presented very seriously by the artists and crew.
It's very easy to fall into parody but Hammer never did that. I guess these films were a way of filtering through the idea of goodness and purity triumphing over evil. They have a curious, almost spiritual quality I suppose.

The Curse of the Werewolf

" I think that my best make-up was the Werewolf with Oliver Reed. I think that was the most satisfactory one, the most rewarding and one of the most difficult. "

The Curse Of The Werewolf Production Details: Released May 1, 1961 (UK), June 7, 1961 (US); 88 Minutes; Technicolor; 7920 Feet; A Hammer-Hot spur Production; A Rank (UK) Universal International (US) Release Filmed at Bray Studios; Director: Terence Fisher; Producer: Anthony Hinds; Executive Producer: Michael Carreras; Associate Producer: Anthony Nelson-Keys; Screenplay: John Elder, Based on Guy Endore's 'The Werewolf of Paris'; Music: Benjamin Frankel; Director of Photography: Arthur Grant; Editor: Alfred Cox; Supervising Editor: James Needs; Production Manager: Clifford Parkes; Sound Recordist: Jock May; Camera: Len Harris; Continuity: Tilly Day; Wardrobe: Molly Arbuthnot; Hairdresser: Freda Steiger; Make-up: Roy Ashton; Art Director: Thomas Goswell; Assistant Art Director: Don Mingaye; Production Design: Bernard Robinson; Assistant Director: John Peverall; Second Assistant: Dominic Fulford; Special Effects: Les Bowie; UK Certificate: X.

Cast List: Clifford Evans (Professor Carrido), Oliver Reed (Leon), Yvonne Romain (Servant Girl), Catherine Feller (Christina), Anthony Dawson (Marquis), Hira Talfrey (Teresa), Richard Wordsworth (Beggar), Francis DeWolff (Landlord), Warren Mitchell (Pepe), George Woodbridge (Dominique), John Gabriel (priest), Ewen Solon (Don Fernando), Peter Sallis (Don Enrique), Michael Ripper (The Old Soak), Sheila Brennan (Vera), Martin Matthews (Jose), David Conville (Gomez), Anne Blake (Rosa), Denis Shaw (The Jailer), Josphine Llewellyn (Marquesa), Justin Walters (Young Leon), Renny Lister (Yvonne), Joy Webster (Isobel), John Bennett (policeman), Charles Lamb (The Chief), Desmond Llewellyn (Footman), Gordon Witting (Second Footman), Hamlyn Benson (Landlord), Serafina DiLeo (Zumara), Kitty Attwood (Midwife), Howard Lang (Irate Farmer), Stephen W Scott (Another Farmer), Max Butterfield (Cheeky Farmer), Ray Brown (Official), Frank Siernan (Gardner), Michael Peake (Farmer in Cantina), Rodney Burke, Alan Page, Richard Golding (Customers), Michael Lewis (Page), Lorraine Caruana (Servant Girl as Child).

The Curse of the Werewolf is often referred to as Roy Ashton's triumph in the art of cinema make-up design. It is certainly his most renowned work. The design for the werewolf itself needed to be done with great sensitivity, as this poor, tortured creature was to be pitied as much as feared. The tragedy of the werewolf was not to be lost, and the make-up design, although terrifyingly suggestive of a ferocious animal, was still essentially a human being. More recent trends toward "realism", relying only on technical effects such as computer graphics and mechanical devices, rather than make-up, are not able to preserve the humanity of such tormented souls. While fascinating to watch, many modern effects overshadow the human performances and fail to use the special effects to develop pathos.

Ashton's original photographs and sketches of a wolf in the Natural History Museum, London.

As with all of his other films, Roy worked as a freelance on "Werewolf". He had heard that Hammer was planning the picture, and went to the studio to obtain a script. He believed that by preparing in advance, he would be more likely to secure the work. He was right. By the time the offer of work came from producer Anthony Nelson Keys, Roy had already done much of the research, and turned up at the studio armed

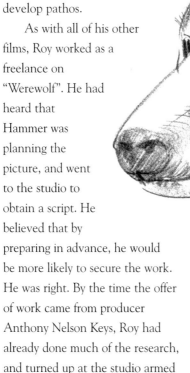

Ashton
was engaged
only to apply
make-up
during the
days of
shooting.

FALCON FILMS LTD.

"HAMMER HOUSE," 113-117 WARDOUR STREET - LONDON - W.I Tel: GERRARD 9787 (10 Lines)
STUDIOS: - DOWN PLACE - WINDSOR - BERKSHIRE   Tel: MAIDENHEAD 2591/2 and 2201
Directors: JAMES CARRERAS, M.B.E.   MICHAEL CARRERAS   M. J. FRANKOVICH (U.S.A.)   L. R. WOOLNER   - ANTHONY HINDS
K. L. MAIDMENT

5th September, 1960.

Roy Ashton, Esq.,
37, South Terrace,
Surbiton,
Surrey.

Dear Mr. Ashton,   re: 'THE CURSE OF THE WEREWOLF'.

I have much pleasure in confirming your engagement
as HEAD OF THE MAKEUP DEPARTMENT on the above mentioned production
for the complete period of the picture, on the following terms
and conditions :-

1. Your engagement will commence on the
    12th September, 1960.

2. You will receive a basic fee of £45.0.0.
    (FORTY-FIVE POUNDS ONLY) per week.

3. The usual terms and conditions of the B.F.P.A./
    N.A.T.K.E. Agreement will be observed at all
    times.

If you are agreeable to the above, will you kindly
sign and return the attached carbon copy of this letter.

Yours sincerely,
BRAY STUDIOS-FALCON FILMS LTD.

Anthony Nelson Keys.
ANTHONY NELSON KEYS.
General Manager.

ANK/vcr.

Read and agreed ....

ALL CORRESPONDENCE TO BE ADDRESSED TO FALCON FILMS LTD.

87

with sketches and ideas. Work started officially for Roy on 12 September 1960, although by that date, all of the make-up designs had been completed.

When I was asked to work on *The Curse of The Werewolf*. Tony Hinds said to me: "Roy, you must get something or other from somewhere about wolves." I said I knew where there was a wolf and I would go and make a drawing of it. So I set off to the Natural History Museum, as there happens to be a big stuffed one in a showcase there. The Natural History Museum and The British Museum are two of my favourite hunting grounds for background information. I took my camera and made some drawings and that was the basis for the make-up in that film. Having read the script, I wanted to have a good idea of a real wolf.

Dozens and dozens of sketches are usually made as a preliminary. The hardest thing is usually to find out what the producers want. To create the wolf like appearance on an actor meant setting up a full sized model and adapting its appearance to a human head.

The studio was uncertain who to cast in the role of the werewolf. Hammer asked Roy's advice on casting for the role.

Tony Hinds asked me: " Who do you suppose we can get?" I suggested Oliver Reed, since he seemed exactly right – his bones and everything. His

powerful bone structure was just right for the appearance and his gifts as an actor were perfect for the part. In addition, he resembles a wolf anyway when he is very angry. I produced a cast of his head and changed it into what I think he would look like as a wolf. Ollie got the part. That is what happened. He was most co-operative, I must say. He was a real professional chap and very ambitious at the time, as this film was his big chance. He would do anything. Nothing was too much trouble. As far as a professional artist goes, I think he was marvellous. He put everything he had into that role, it was a great performance.

How this werewolf make-up was created has been the question most frequently asked of Roy. He never refused to give a patient and detailed answer.

Ashton examines his

werewolf from

every angle.

The werewolf makeup is a highly complicated process. First of all you have got to reproduce the actor's head. That means casting and moulding. You cast his head and reproduce it in plaster. The changes that you hope to make you model either in wax or plasticine, then you have to reproduce the change. I made an appliance which fitted underneath his eyes and went right over the top of his head and over the ears. I pushed out his nostrils with a pair of candles. I used walnuts first of all. You cut a walnut in half, punch a hole through the shell, and stick it up the nostril. It's a bit uncomfortable. But if you take a candle and draw the wick out of it, then that leaves you with a sort of hollow cylinder. I cut sections off of that and stick them up the artist's nose and the warmth of the nose adjusts the shape of the candle to the shape of the nostrils. Then you can breathe easily and it doesn't irritate the nose. I made the eyebrows up a little more massively as well. Then you have got to make teeth and heaven only knows what and at the back of the neck, a dog makes some very characteristic movements which needed to be reproduced on this wolf-like person. I made a series of beards which I fastened around the neck so that they just slipped around there when the artist moved. A succession of hair falls, rather like overlapping sheathes, were fitted to the back of the neck and towards the shoulders. The main trunk was fitted with a leotard and Yak hair was put all over this to simulate the coat of

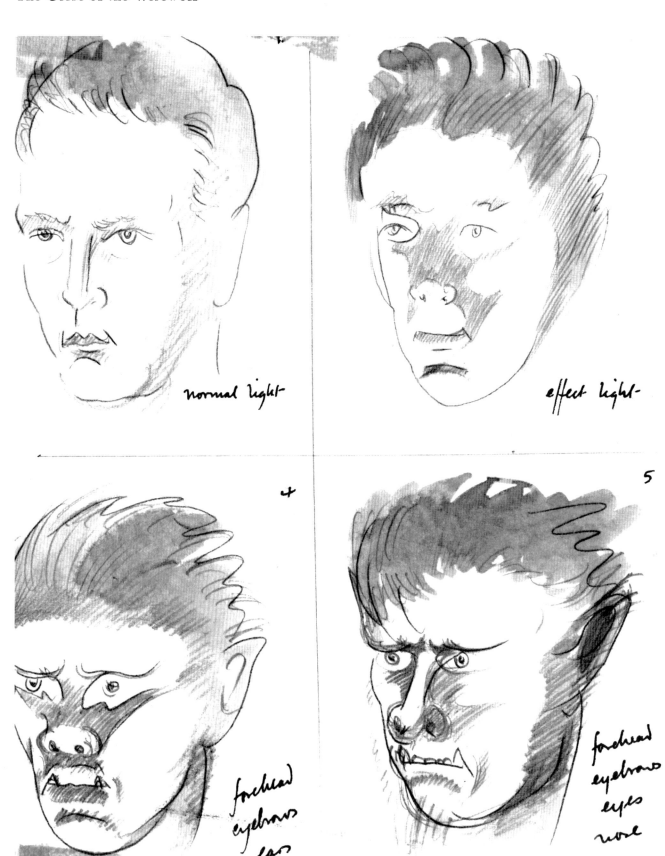

normal light

effect light

forehead
eyebrows
ears

forehead
eyebrows
eyes
nose

90

Ashton's suggestion for lighting the transformation from man to wolf.

a wolf. The hands were covered on the back with coarse hair. The fingernails were extended to suggest claws. Contact lenses were inserted for extreme close shots. Teeth were extended – canines made and fitted. It was quite a complicated job. It took about an hour and a half to two hours. I was hardly ever off the set where Oliver Reed's makeup was concerned.

Elizabeth Ashton:

"Oliver Reed's friend, Phil Rasmussen, happens to be a dental surgeon, and like Roy, an Australian. He accompanied Oliver to Bray and started to talk to Roy. Phil pointed out that Roy really shouldn't be taking impressions of teeth to make the fangs

Leon the WEREWOLF

Sequence F.

Character No 9

Sc. 150 — onwards
Young boy. 9 yrs. does not change

Sequence G.

Stage 1

The werewolf was
Character No.9 in
Ashton's sketchbook.

Scs. 282

Stage 2 1. forehead & ears

2. teeth

3. contact lenses

Stage 3   1. forehead
2. eyes
3. ears
4. teeth

Sc. 403 - 405

Ashton suggested Oliver Reed for the role.

for the werewolf. He gave Roy a few hints on how to make fangs and so on.

The relationship between Roy and Phil Rasmussen developed into a friendship, and Rasmussen worked with Roy on several other films where complex dental appliances needed to be developed."

Oliver Reed:

"No one would sit next to me in the studio canteen. Even the waitress used to eye me strangely and keep at a distance. I am not surprised. I was scared myself when I saw the rush shots with blood trickling from my mouth and down my clothes and my nostrils plugged up to make them enlarged, and my face made up in a terrifying fashion. I looked a gory mess."

Jackie Cooper (Oliver Reed's stunt double):

"With the Werewolf they put it on as soon as you got there – seven o'clock in the morning. It took two and a half hours to put on. It wasn't very comfortable. Most of it was in already prepared pieces, glued onto your face and then they layered hair onto of it over your own skin. Around the mouth it was very uncomfortable – you couldn't eat anything. They didn't put anything up my nostrils, they put it on top of my nose. I had

Ashton's meticulous attention to the werewolf's hand.

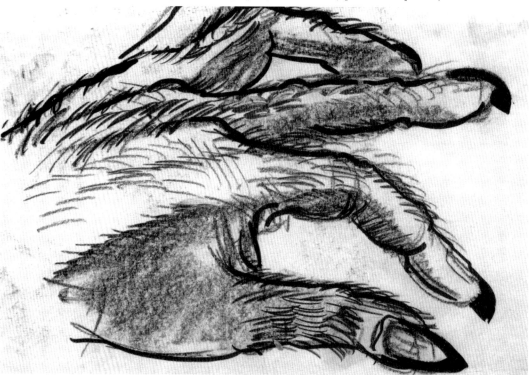

to wear fangs in my mouth but not contact lenses, where they were doing close-ups they needed all that other stuff but with a long shot that wasn't thought necessary. I did all the running about on the roof tops, hanging outside the bell tower and climbing into it. I couldn't have too many make-up appliances because it was too much of an hindrance."

Roy was busy making up the male and female leads. I didn't really see him much on that picture. Colin Guard was the technician who applied my make-up. The design of the Werewolf make-up was brilliant in itself. The make-up room was lined with photographs and drawings, so that it would be the same every day. One day, Oliver Reed and I stood together and had photographs taken. I don't think there was any difference between how we looked, except maybe Oliver was a little taller.

Some people have commented on the similarity of my make-up to Jack Pierce's in *The Werewolf of London* or Jean Cocteau's *La Belle et la Bête*. I've never seen either picture, though.

The transformation scenes create difficulties more for the camera people than the make-up people. We can take the artist away after fixing their position in the scene by means of clamps or blocks. I suggested the wolfman's transformation by only showing his hands. To do this we had to lock them off in the same position for each shot of the stop-motion photography: I prepared a cast

The werewolf's head took pride of place in Ashton's drying cupboard.

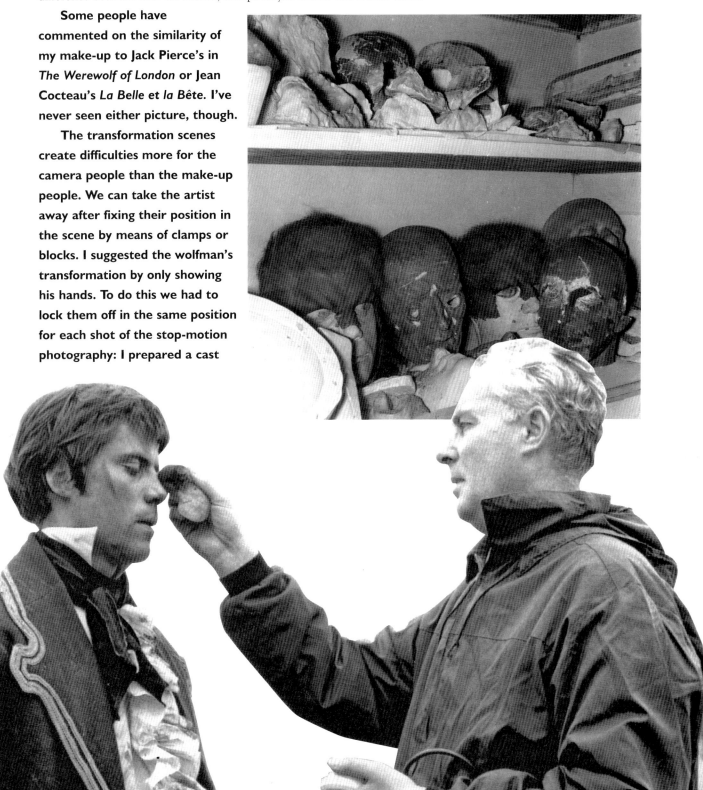

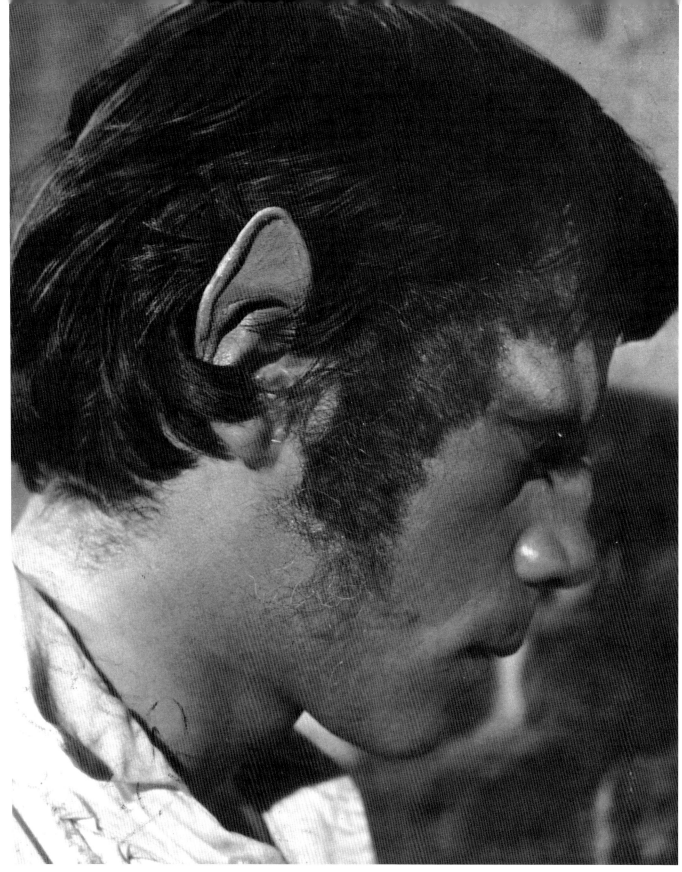

Oliver Reed in
transformation.

out of plaster with their imprints, so that every time they stopped the camera we could take Oliver away to apply more hair and to make the nails a little longer. When he came back he put his hand in the cast again, as it had been before. Roughly speaking, this is what it was: the whole treatment took about two hours.

The Curse of the Werewolf contains two other complex character make-ups. Ashton's designs for the Beggar (Richard Wordsworth), provides a three-stage transformation from a starving vagabond to a hirsute beast. Roy's notes query the

THE BEGGAR
CHARACTER 2.

Sequence "A"
1. Own hair if long enough
2. unshaven
3. hollow with shading

Sequence "B"

1. Large unkempt beard
2. wig
3. coarse hair on body
4. enlarged lower teeth?

....

Character sheet for the Beggar suggests teeth and claws not used in the film.

Sequence "C"

1. even more hairy
2. hands .. / claws (?)

filthy - crazy.

To BE MADE
a. Coarse dark wig
b. beard & moustache
c. teeth (?)

THE BEGGAP

inclusion of fangs and claws. It was a controversy raised by the British censors, who insisted that all overt references combining sexual intercourse with supernatural beings had to be removed.

Richard Wordsworth:

"Just before shooting began, I had come to get fitted with fangs but nobody at the studio seemed to know anything about them. Finally I found someone who did and he told me: "No fangs. The censor says no fangs. You can't have fangs and have relations with the girl as well." Well, the character played by Oliver Reed had to be 'born' so they obviously chose relations with the girl. We were just about to start the scene where I attack the girl when Terence Fisher turned to the property man and said "Have you got the white of an egg?" I asked him: "Er, what's this white of egg for?" "Oh this is something we always do", he said. "You have a mouthful of egg white and when you see the girl just slobber a little of it. But keep it tasteful."

The Marquis Siniestro (Anthony Dawson), carried a reminder of every wicked deed and sordid practice he had engaged in since imprisoning the Beggar. Similar to his work on *The Man Who Could Cheat Death*, Roy's make-up design explored his fascination with the graphic portrayal of the effects of debauchery and old age on evil characters. It is unclear who suggested that Dawson should pick bits of his skin off his

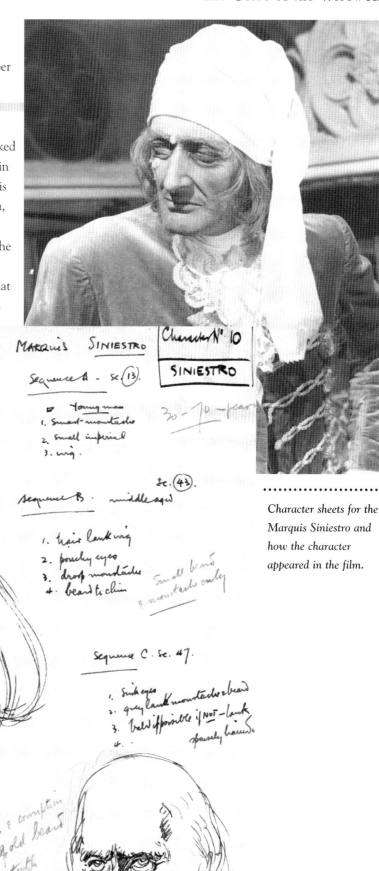

Character sheets for the Marquis Siniestro and how the character appeared in the film.

face in an attempt to improve his appearance for the chamber-maid, but this disgusting trait augmented Roy's design extremely well.

Roy's work on *Curse of the Werewolf* officially terminated on 2 November 1960. He was paid £436 for eight weeks work, inclusive of consummable material costs. Roy was not paid for the weeks of preparation he had invested before 12 September. In addition, there was no payment or mention of the design copyright for the werewolf; a situation quite different from what would have been today, where complex legal contracts and recompense for copyright ensure ownership by the studio.

> **I don't like it as a film, to be quite frank. In a way this was a disgusting story... Why? Well, the wicked squire and his cronies all misbehave in a terrible fashion on his wedding night. In comes a beggar and they think they could have some fun with this man, not by giving him food, but by offering him plenty of wine. They succeed in making him drunk so that he starts dancing and gets a bit above himself, unwillingly insulting his host. Thereupon he is thrown in the dungeons, where he languishes for twenty-five years. At the end of this period he becomes a terrible object, not having washed or shaved, living on scraps and bones, sleeping on straw. In the course of time the marquis, who is still up to his old tricks, tries to have his way with the housemaid, yet she resists: she is punished by being locked up in the prison with this pitiable thing down there, who rapes her and dies in the act of violation. She then gets out, grabs something sharp and stabs the squire to death. Running off and trying to do away with herself by jumping in the river, she is saved by a kind scholar but expires in giving birth to her son. This product of the union in jail is a werewolf, a young boy who, when the moon is full, goes out into the night, baying at the moon and worrying sheep, and getting the taste of blood... Now really: if this isn't an awful affair!**

The Phantom of the Opera

The Phantom of the Opera Released June 25, 1962 (U.K.), August 15, 1962 (U.S.); 84 minutes (U.K.), 94 minutes (U.S. Television); Technicolor (U.K.), Eastmancolor (U.S.); 7560 feet; a Hammer Film Production; a Rank Organisation Release (U.K.), a Universal Release (U.S.); filmed at Bray Studios, England; Director: Terence Fisher; Producer: Anthony Hinds; Associate Producer: Basil Keys; Screenplay: John Elder, based on the story by Gaston Leroux; Director of Photography: Arthur Grant; Art Directors: Bernard Robinson, Don Mingaye; Supervising Editor: James Needs; Editor: Alfred Cox; Music Composed and Conducted by: Edwin Astley; Makeup: Roy Ashton; Production Manager: Clifford Parkes; Costumes: Molly Arbuthnot; Camera: Len Harris; 1st Assistant Director: John Peverall; 2nd Assistant Director: Peter Medac; Continuity: Tilly Day; Sound: Jock May; Hairdresser: Frieda Steiger; Wardrobe Mistress: Rosemary Burrows; Stills Camera: Tom Edwards; Sound Editor: James Groom; Sound Recordist: Jock May; Opera Scenes Staged by Dennis Maunder; U.K. Certificate: A.

Herbert Lom (The Phantom/Petrie), Edward de Souza (Harry Hunter), Heather Sears (Christine Charles), Michael Gough (Lord Ambrose D'Arcy), Thorley Walters (Lattimer), Ian Wilson (Dwarf), Martin Miller (Rossi), John Harvey (Sgt. Vickers), Miles Malleson (Philosophical Cabby), Marne Maitland (Xavier), Michael Ripper (Long Faced Cabby), Patrick Troughton (Rat Catcher), Renee Houston (Mrs. Tucker), Sonya Cordeau (Yvonne), Liane Aukin (Matria), Leila Forde (Teresa), Geoff L'Oise (Frenchman), Miriam Karlin (Charwoman), Harold Goodwin (Bill), Keith Pyott (Weaver). Cast for U.S. Television added footage: Liam Redmond (Police Inspector), John Maddison (Police Inspector).

"For *The Phantom of The Opera* I consulted all previous versions and deliberately started my conception away from them. But you must remember that the make-up artist is engaged to carry out the wishes of the employers..."

When Roy Ashton heard that Hammer was planning to do the cinema's third version of Gaston Leroux's novel, *Phantom of the Opera* (1908), he responded enthusiastically. He loved designing period make-up, and his first love was Opera. Even more importantly, the original version of this film with Lon Chaney had had a profound effect on him, Chaney was to be his enduring inspiration.

I remember seeing that back in Australia when I was quite young, and to me, Chaney's make-up was one of the most remarkable things I'd ever seen. At the crucial point where the girl removes his mask, I can still remember the scream the audience gave. It was a terrific scene!

"'Suddenly I wanted desperately to see beneath the mask. I wanted to know the face of the voice and, with a movement which I was utterly unable to control, my fingers swiftly tore away the mask. Oh horror, horror, horror!'"

From *Phantom of the Opera* by Gaston Leroux

Resplendent with masks and effects, the lavish 1925 Universal release was the first time Roy witnessed the power of cinema to shock an audience. Absorbed by Chaney's

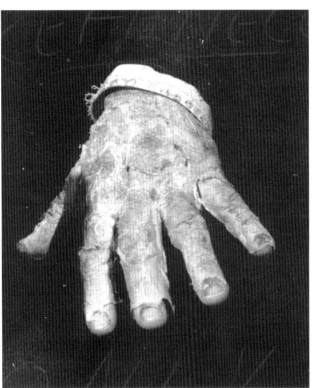

performance, Roy recalled how at the unmasking sequence in the original film, three small boys were perched on the back of their seats. Clinging to each other for support the shocking sight of Chaney's lidless eyes and rancid teeth caused the boys to panic and fall backwards into the audience.

The original story was of a lone musician tortured by his quest for artistic perfection. The mysterious Erik is tremendously wealthy through his intrigues in Persia. Isolated from society because of his congenital ugliness, he wears a mask and hides beneath the Paris Opera House. Creating beautiful music is his all consuming passion. The Phantom's dilemma is that to be appreciated art must be shared with others. Erik hates society and decides to kidnap a beautiful soprano to share his underground kingdom.

As usual, Roy was obsessed with factual detail. He would create an original approach based on meticulous research, starting with descriptions in Leroux's novel.

"He is extraordinarily thin and his dress-coat hangs on a skeleton frame. His eyes are so deep set that you can hardly see the pupils. All you see is two big black holes, as in a dead man's skull. His skin, which is stretched across his bones like a drumhead, is a dirty yellow. He has hardly any nose to speak of and the only hair he has is three or four long dark locks on his forehead and behind the ears."

from *Phantom of the Opera* by Gaston Leroux

Research meant a broadening of my work into hitherto unknown realms of experimenting with materials, anatomical peculiarities and the wonders of

science. The story writer has an easy approach through that vast field of the imagination. But when it comes to applying the fruits of those exotic thought processes you have to get down to brass tacks and deliver what the imagination has suggested. I will acknowledge a night or two without sleep. Little did those writers realise the technical problems necessary to give expression in picture form to those odd and impossible situations which they airily describe. I imagine the solutions I offered were acceptable to my employers, otherwise I would not have remained long in my situation as head of that particular department.

Roy began experimenting with ideas based on the effects of hydrochloric acid on human tissue. He quite liked the idea of a half melted face, such as might be the result of intense radiation. He remembered the photos he had seen of the effects of the Hiroshima bomb, and wished to reproduce the same hideous scarring. However, once again, the producers at Hammer were concerned about cost and time. They told Roy to keep the deformity simple, as they did not intend to feature it as Chaney did in the original. Tony Hinds wrote "We didn't use Roy's make-up because we thought it was probably too much". Roy was heartbroken. This was a make-up he badly wanted to do. All that is left of his original and spectacular intentions is the sketches he made.

Roy always sketched designs based on the actor's face. The sketches of the Phantom/Professor Petrie character is clearly not Herbert Lom, suggesting that he had not yet been cast. This supports the initial Tony Hinds' story that Herbert Lom was a late choice for the role, as Cary Grant was under consideration (from an interview in *Fangoria* 74). Hinds has recently contradicted his earlier story. "Lom did not replace Grant!", Hinds told the authors in a recent communication. Although the facts are now shrouded in mystery, Roy's drawings are evidence that Lom was not cast as of 2 December 1961, eleven days after filming had actually begun. The producers had not yet decided what the Phantom should look like.

Roy thoroughly enjoyed working with Herbert Lom.

The acid burning appearance was the result of consulting technical as well as medical books and from actual observations of such mishaps. Herbert Lom is a marvellously co-operative artist who I have encountered on many subsequent films for Amicus also upon the versions of *The Pink Panther*.

Herbert Lom used to converse with Roy about philosophy and spiritual matters. Roy remembered an evening out with Herbert Lom some years later in Hong Kong, while working on one of the Pink Panther films.

I was invited to supper by a prominent member of our cast, Herbert Lom. He had in his own country been a member of a very wealthy family, who were accustomed to entertaining world famous artists until the Russian domination. He had a longing to discuss music which he knew at one time

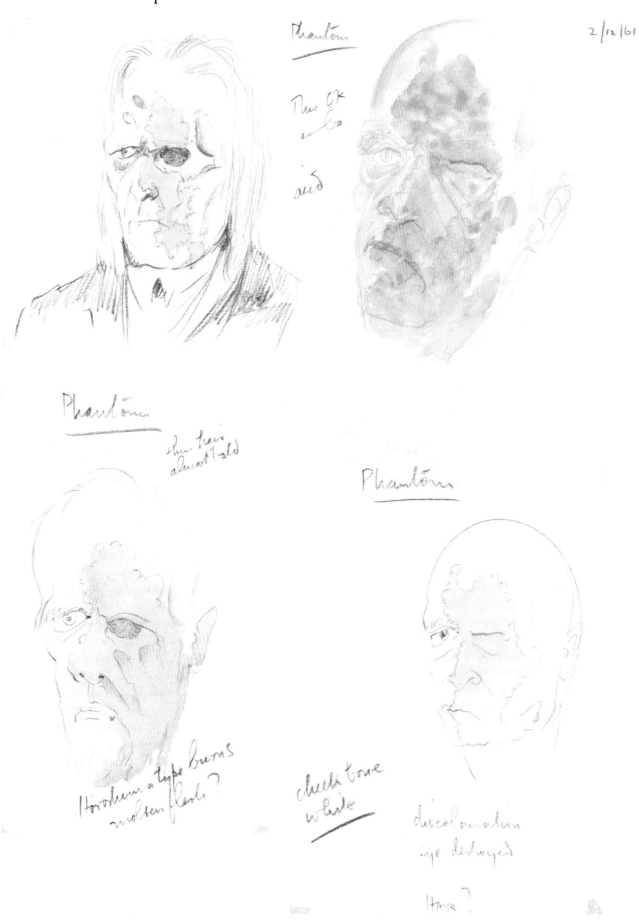

had been my profession. Seated in an elegant restaurant, the bill of fare I knew would cost a king's ransom. I left the ordering to my host. It was interesting to hear his comments on so many great artists, musically and socially.

Herbert Lom:

"Roy Ashton was the kind of make-up artist who made you feel completely relaxed and unworried regarding your make-up; even when it was a question of sculpting complicated masks, etc. which he did for me in *Phantom of the Opera* (1962). This feeling of ease and relaxation he succeeded in "imposing" onto the hysterical occupants of his make-up chair was only possible, I think, because he was such an exceptional expert and such a devoted and charming person himself."

After the efforts to design a mask for the Phantom by a professional mask designer failed to please the producers, Roy was asked to come up with an idea. Perhaps this was meant as a consolation from the studio which was stifling his creativity. Roy was equally meticulous about the Phantom's mask. Once again, he sought inspiration in reference books.

About six weeks before the picture was due to go into production, the question of the mask arose. At the recommendation of the art department, Tony Hinds had called upon a mask maker to come up with something suitable for the Phantom to wear. He was responsible for a number of designs, some of which I saw, that were beautiful. Nevertheless, they were not what was requested and the make-up section had to fill in some ideas as usual. My suggestion was that the Phantom, almost certainly, would have picked up some mask from the theatre properties to conceal his features. Something readily available, because he wouldn't be able to go into shops or anything like that: it wouldn't matter very much what it was, it only had to be distinctive and immediately recognisable. I thought about old Japanese masks as they were pictured in a sumptuous publication entitled "Masks of the World", which I found in the Victoria and Albert Museum. I invited Tony Hinds to come and have a look, but he told me he couldn't spare

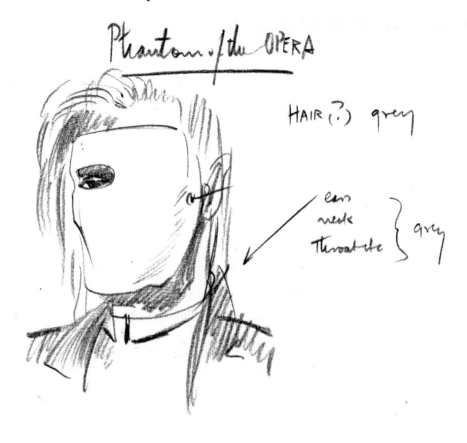

Phantom of the OPERA

HAIR (?) grey

ears
neck
throat etc } grey

Sc. 55 (a) yellow bloodshot
CONTACT LENS ?

disfigurement — where ?
natural colours to show
when domino mask is worn .

HANDS ?

grey — Knotted, arthritic — veins

STAFF ? EXTRA needed

the time. So I made a few drawings and showed them to him, but it was not exactly what he hoped for. I next appeared with a book of Japanese Kabuki masks. "That is not bad," he uttered when seeing one of them and he tore the page out, pushing a hole through it. "He's got to look out of one of these, hasn't he ?", he waved away my objection that this was not a way to treat

Phantom

when concealed — what mark?
something taken from Theatre properties?

This is Japanese — one eye socket ripped out.

literature. Still he couldn't make up his mind, even when they began shooting the film. Three weeks later we were in the theatre where they had to photograph Herbert Lom with his mask on, and no decision had been taken yet. "Look," I said, "give me five minutes and I will make you one." I got an old piece of rag, tied it round his face, cut a hole in it, stuck a little bit of

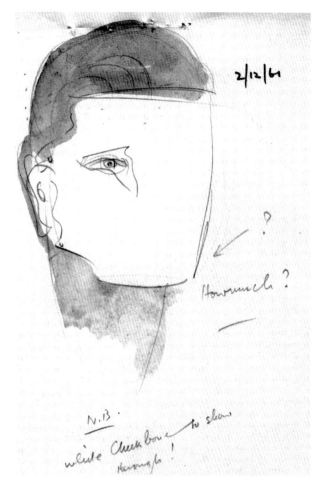

2/12/4

N.B.
white Cheek bone to show
through !

How much ?

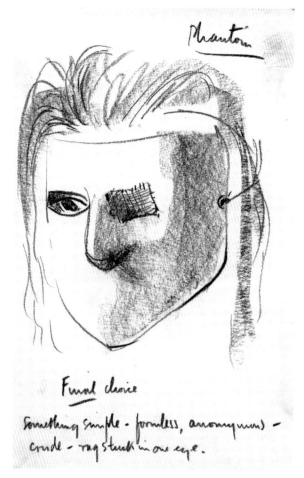

Phantom

Final choice

Something simple - formless, anonymous -
crude - rag stuck in one eye.

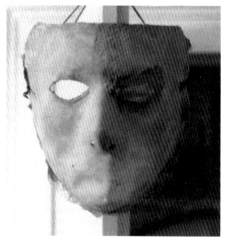

mesh over one of the eyes, two bits of string around it, and tried it. "Great!" they cried out, "that is just what we want!" Later I strengthened it, and that is what they used in *The Phantom of the Opera*. I often laugh when I think back to that: only a piece of nothing after having had a professional artist there for six weeks, books, and God knows what!

The Wimbledon Theatre was the location for the finale of the film, and the setting for the scenes where the Phantom would be unmasked. The finished make-up was seen only fleetingly on Herbert Lom. It was stunt double Jackie Cooper who was subjected to terrible scarring for the leap from the box to the stage. The make-up was designed and tested on Jackie Cooper, as Lom's time was expensive, and the make-up tests which Roy had saved show the make-up in a degree of detail not seen in the film.

Jackie Cooper (Hammer stunt man and Herbert Lom's double):

"One job at Hammer I enjoyed was to double for Herbert Lom in *The Phantom Of The Opera*. I don't think I ever saw him actually. I've seen him a lot since. I didn't know much about the business and I just got on with the job. They built up a sewer on the set and they had tippers there gushing the water down and I was washed down the sewer.

It wasn't a really difficult gag to do because I had just come out of the Aqua-shows. I had started as a high diver and anything with water for me was quite easy. I only had

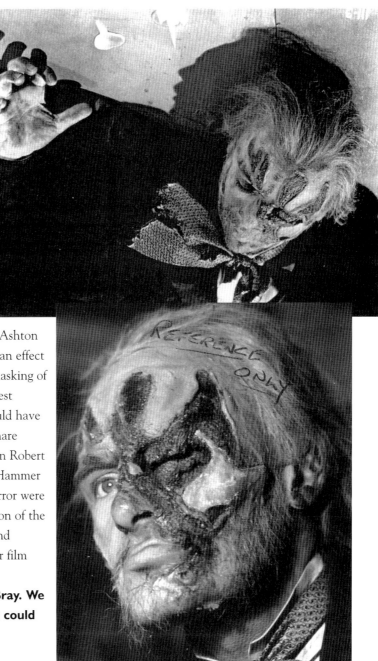

half of my face made-up. I've never really had any problems with the make-up I've been asked to wear.

There was a leap in Wimbledon Theatre. I was off onto the stage, that wasn't very high – it was only 10-12 foot out of a box. Usually it was one take. They didn't mess about with stunts in those days."

Hammer's version was released in 1962. It never really approached the true horror of the Chaney original. The Phantom's make-up and unmasking fell short as Roy Ashton was to admit later. His chance of creating an effect as startling as Chaney's was lost. The unmasking of Chaney remains one of the cinema's greatest moments. With Roy Ashton, Hammer could have equalled that moment, but they did not share Roy's enthusiasm. Indeed, cinema historian Robert Murphy writes, "Critics who condemned Hammer for its supposed emphasis on gruesome horror were lukewarm in supporting this reinterpretation of the old melodrama as a romantic love story, and cinemagoers who had come to see a horror film were disappointed by its lack of thrills."

We didn't have the resources at Bray. We were very limited. And the producers could never make up their minds.

Roy saved those original designs, and sometimes showed them to fans almost apologetically, as if to say "It wasn't my fault. This is how the Phantom should have looked."

 The make-up for the Phantom wasn't very complicated. A great deal of pieces, with the wrinkled flesh and everything, had been manufactured beforehand. The final application required nothing more than some adjustment, the trimming of edges etc. That was all.

The Evil of Frankenstein

The Evil Of Frankenstein
Production Details:
Released May 31, 1964(UK),
May 8, 1964 (US); 84 Minutes;
Eastmancolor;
A Hammer Film Production;
A Rank Organisation Release
(UK), Universal Release (US);
Filmed at Bray Studios;
Director: Freddie Francis;
Producer: Anthony Hinds;
Screenplay: John Elder;
Music: Don Banks;
Music Supervisor: John
Hollingsworth;
Director of Photography:
John Wilcox;
Supervising Editor:
James Needs;
Editor: Chris Barnes;
Production Manager:
Don Weeks;
Sound Recordist: Ken Rawkins;
Camera: Ronnie Maasz;
Continuity: Pauline Harlow;
Wardrobe: Rosemary Burrows;
Hairdresser: Frieda Steiger;
Make-Up: Roy Ashton;
Art Director: Don Mingaye;
Production Design:
Bernard Robinson;
Assistant Director: Bill
Cartlidge;
Special Effects: Bowie Films
Ltd.; UK Certificate: X.

Cast:
Peter Cushing (Baron
Frankenstein),
Peter Woodthorpe (Zoltan),
Sandor Eles (Hans),
Duncan Lamont (Chief of
Police),
Katy Wild (Beggar Girl),
Kiwi Kingston (The Creature)

> **Unlike *The Curse of Frankenstein* we were no longer under any copyright restrictions regarding the creature's appearance. However, Hammer did not want a direct copy of the Jack Pierce make-up. To tell the truth they didn't really know what they wanted.**

The Evil of Frankenstein

The *Curse Of Frankenstein* (1957) and *Revenge Of Frankenstein* (1958), represented Hammer's first forays into this classic tale of Gothic horror. The copyright restrictions on the Jack Pierce make-up, used by Universal Pictures, forced then make-up chief Phil Leakey, to explore new and innovative conceptions for the creature. Later dealings between Hammer and Universal resulted in a lifting of the ban. Free to use a variation of the make-up for Karloff, Hammer faced a critical choice. They could continue with the original Leakey concept, encourage Roy Ashton to provide a new presentation, or pursue a slavish clone of Universal's Monster. A distribution deal struck with Universal, forced the studio into the latter course of action.

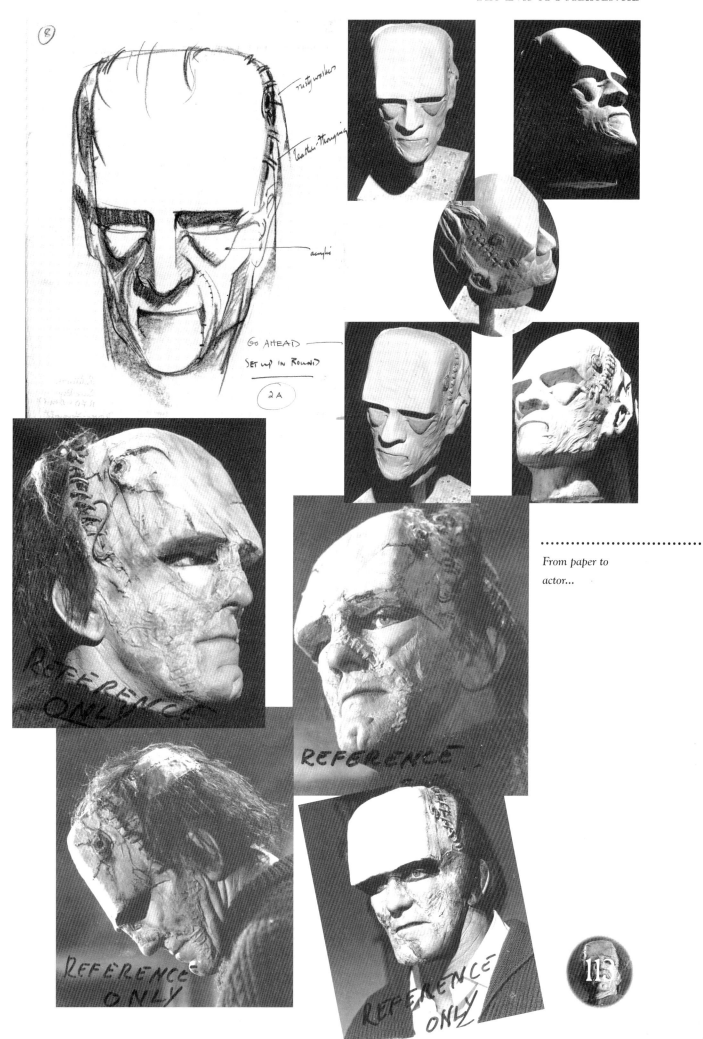

From paper to actor...

113

Also, part of this decision may have had to do with the fact that their "Frankenstein" director, Terry Fisher was not short-listed for this new project. Following the commercial disaster of *The Phantom of the Opera*, Hammer enlisted Freddie Francis.

Freddie Francis:

"Tony Hinds who ran Hammer with Sir James Carreras would say: 'Lets make another Frankenstein film.' Tony Hinds is a very dear friend of mine so I mustn't speak badly of him. No, I mustn't say that, I will speak badly of him. Because when I do

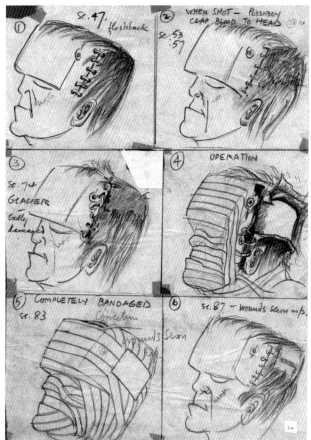

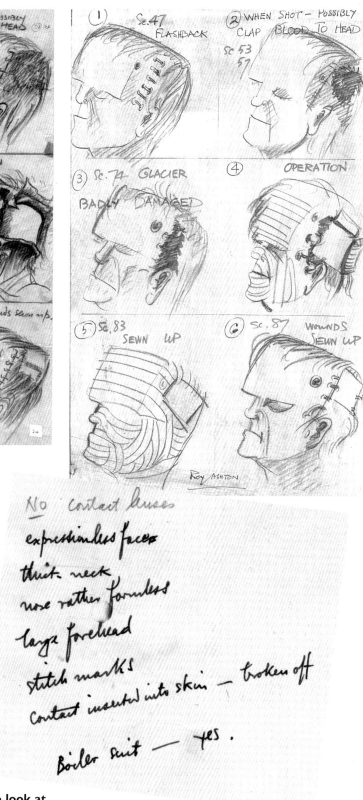

lectures and things I'm always saying what a wonderful organisation it was. If I was asked to go on a film a month before it started shooting, that was a long time. And before they even approached me, they had approached somebody like Roy Ashton and Jimmy Sangster. All I knew about the make-up was that they had received permission from Universal to use the Jack Pierce make-up, which they hadn't been allowed to use for the previous two Frankensteins"

Jack Pierce! He's one of the pioneers. I knew Mr. Karloff with whom I worked in England and he had the greatest admiration for Jack Pierce. I think all make-up artists feel the same. We never miss an opportunity to look at stills of his work and marvel at his skill in handling the materials which were then generally in use. However whilst working at Hammer I always tried my own ideas. The appearance of a very crude operation on the cranium to insert the brain and a none-too successful sewing up of bits of skin and bone perhaps with string was thought to have good entertainment value (by the management) however ludicrous from a surgeon's point of view.

Contrary to the Press Book, Roy Ashton actually produced almost 200 different

Roy plans changes to the creature make-up scene by scene

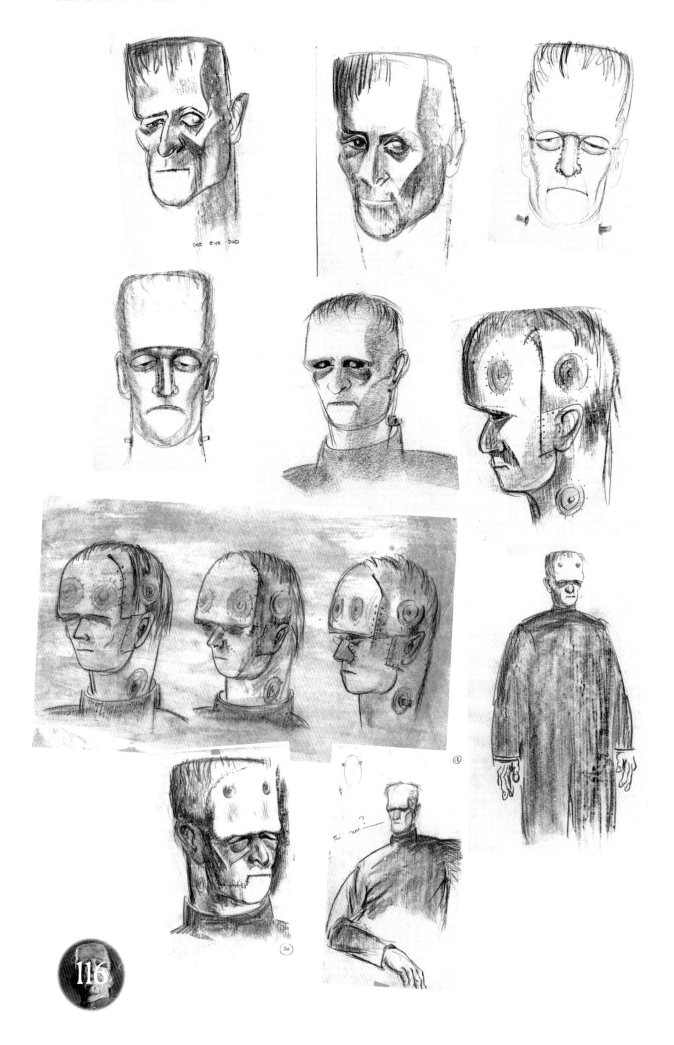

116

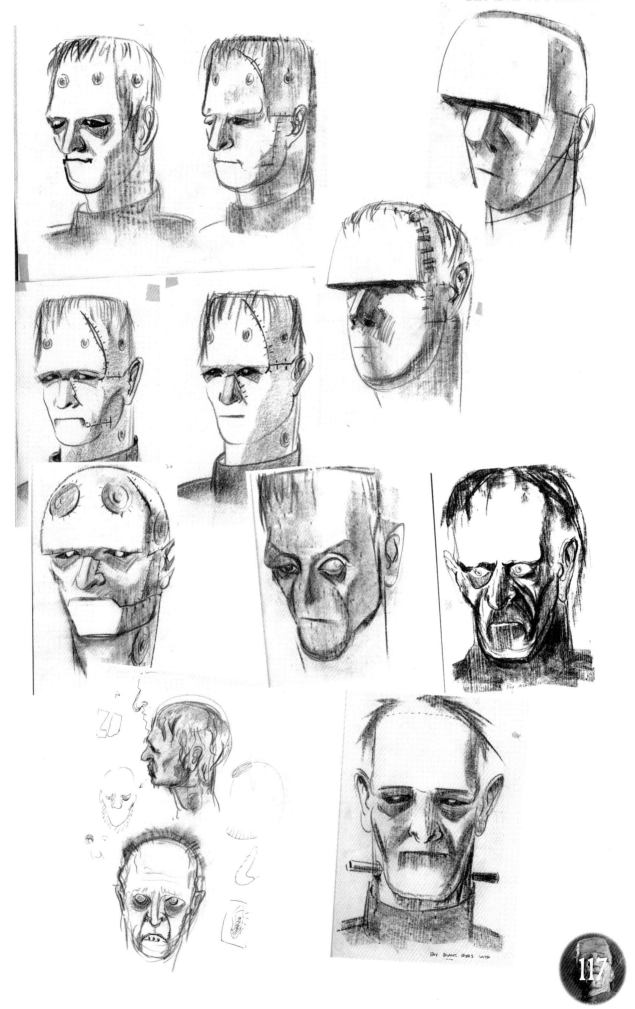

117

ideas for the Creature. He worked like a man possessed for several weeks, without pay, before his actual engagement on *The Evil of Frankenstein* was to commence. He became totally immersed in the challenge of developing a new look for the most famous monster of all time.

I began work about a month before the first shooting day. I drew dozens and dozens of suggestions. I must have completed nearly two hundred drawings for them to try and narrow down their ideas for something definite. I also made many models for that film as well. It was very difficult indeed to get the management to accept ideas. I documented the whole process involved in creating a new look for the creature, with stage by stage sketches and later with still photographs. I started numbering my drawings. I got up to 120 drawings and then I started throwing them away because it was almost impossible to get the producers of the films to agree about what I should do. When I finally got them to agree about something or other to do with an acceptable design, then I would set up the model full size. The management couldn't make up there minds.

Freddie Francis:

"Those drawings were not made for me to look at. I can't remember ever seeing them before. But that was Roy. I'm sure that there are lots of other Hammer directors that you can show them things like this and they would say 'I didn't know Roy had done this.' I must speak to Tony Hinds, who as you know was the producer of all those films and ask him if he had ever seen them. I suspect that not even Tony had seen these things. I suspect that good old Roy, God bless him, had gone ahead and worked his butt off doing these, before Tony told him: 'Oh by the way we are going to use the Universal make-up.' I think it was a pity that they didn't use some of Roy's designs, because going back to the original wasn't all that good an idea."

Top: The plaster cast of Kiwi Kingston's head, upon which make-up was fitted.
Above: Roy sculpted a small model of the creature as a keepsake.

I had been modelling the Monster's head, which is a very time-consuming business, and coming back I found a large gouge right across the top of the forehead, half an inch deep. I was furious. Well, a little later on, Tony Hinds and Freddie Francis simply stepped in and said: "We are sorry we did that,

but we wondered what the effect would be if we had a great big groove there. 'Thanks very much,' I replied, 'it only took me about three days to get this one ready.' Now, as they had approved the basic structure, which was very square, I had actually made the foundation: I had cast and moulded it. And then they asked: 'Do you think you could round it off a bit?' Another few days of hard labour to do! They just didn't realise how long such a process requires.

The management had screen tests before they accepted the artist for the role of the creature. My idea was that the applicants should lumber about before the camera and I suggested that they wear leaded deep sea diver's boots which are very heavy things and restricted their movements to some degree. This made walking difficult, and seemed the best way to suggest a ponderous, pitiful, shambling, slow witted creature.

Freddie Francis had the idea of bringing in this big chap, Kiwi Kingston, to appear as the creature. He was about six feet tall and massively built. Kiwi was a splendid athlete in all forms - boxing, rowing, wrestling. So the physical bulk was already there, so to speak. They picked a very good man for the role. Once they had chosen the artist concerned I was able to proceed further by reproducing Kiwi's head in plaster. Then I tried out the effects upon that. The finished design was a composite of ideas.

I suggested that they should have very loose fitting clothing on him made out of old bags, which they sewed up roughly together. After a time I became more experienced in applying the make-up and I contrived to get it into a single piece, which I pulled around his head sewed up the back then covered it over yet again with the appropriate hair and scar tissue.

Roy's sketch of The Creature in ice.

The top of the forehead and the cheeks were made with paper, the rough patch on top was once a piece of scrap rag. The electrodes were made from two old washers and wires rescued from an old bottle. The operation is sewn up with an old boot lace and string. Latex binds it all in place.

The hands should also express his character, knobbly knuckles and coarse veins can quickly be made with household tissues and mending wool, the sort used for darning socks. I followed the veins in Kiwi's own hands and wrists as a pattern and stuck the strands of wool into position. Over these strands I laid the tissues, putting them down with a damp sponge or a wet paint brush. I covered the lot with latex. A touch of colour heightened the effect.

By short-circuiting some of the steps I finally cut down the application time of the make-up. Instead of taking two and a half to three hours on this blessed thing, I could do it in about half an hour. This included making up the hands, which saved a vast amount of time and energy and worry on the part of the artist. It saved myself time too: instead of having to get there at five in the morning, I could arrive at six!

Freddie Francis:

"Kiwi Kingston didn't 'emote' a great deal. He was a big fellow and he was a lovely guy. I remember that he had to go over, escaping from something and there was a glass case full of keys, and he had to go back and go over, smash the glass and take a key out. So he did this C-R-A-S-H! Out came the key. 'Fine! Cut it!' I said: 'That doesn't quite look right, Kiwi. Would you like to do it again?' Then I saw his hand covered in blood and shouted: 'Get the first aid!' He said, 'No! That's alright. Lets do it again.' And he'd just smashed his hand in the thing. He was a lovely guy to work with. I don't know what happened to Kiwi, he just disappeared. He was a very very sweet person, considering that he was an all-in wrestler. He could have acted better - but there you are!"

For one sequence Freddie wanted Kiwi to bung his hand through a glass panel and he asked me to think of a way we could it safely. Even the specially manufactured sugar frosted glass takes a bit of breaking and the problem really taxed me. Suddenly, I had an idea, I knew there was a piece of tin in the make-up department. I ran up the stairs into one of the workshops and borrowed a pair of tin-snips. I made an enclosure which resembled a clenched hand out of the metal plate and packed it with sponge plastic so that this shield wouldn't injure Kiwi's knuckles. On the outside of the metal I fashioned a set of rubber knuckles and so on which resembled the Creature's clenched fist. This particular problem had occurred to Freddie whilst he was shooting. Usually they have a pre-production conference where all the participants sit around the table and

they go through the script from beginning to end and everyone is invited to
contribute to the ideas in the film. But this extra piece of action was
Freddie's idea. They were holding up the film until I could come up with
something, so I was running from one place to another. That was one
of the wonderful ways they worked at Hammer.
Everyone worked as a team. If I
had some idea which
I thought could
maybe be of use to
the Property
Department it was
welcomed. Nobody
there was jealous of
anyone else's position.
That was the way in
which Hammer worked –
sheer teamwork!

    Despite his retrospective
musings about Bray esprit de
corps, Roy must have been
exasperated about the lack of
commitment to an effective
presentation of the new Creature.
Surely, the "look" of the Creature
in a Frankenstein film was of
primary importance to commercial
and critical success. Of the nearly
200 individual designs Roy had
prepared, most were better than the
one the producers chose. Many of
these never before seen designs are
being presented here for the first time.
Any of these could have had an
amazing presence on the screen, and we
invite you to assess this for yourself. Roy
knew the design chosen didn't actually
work, but always understood his role to
deliver what Hammer asked of him. And
he did so, quite expertly, time and time
again. On this occasion, though, the critical
disapproval was wrongly directed at him.
Examine any book on horror films, and you
will find that there is a preoccupation with the
failure of this Ashton make-up: 'Here's a Roy
Ashton design for a creature and its bad isn't it?'. Roy had heard people say this to his
face. In the first interview he ever gave to Richard Klemensen for the fanzine *Little
Shoppe of Horrors*, Roy responded angrily to Klemensen innocently describing *The Evil*

Of Frankenstein as a failure in terms of his make-up contribution. Imagine how Roy felt about these things when he didn't have the final say? He would show Hammer pages and pages of notes and drawings and the producer would say "that's all very interesting, Roy, but you got a day to sort this out, and you'll never do something like this in a day, so do something simple." We hope that his record of Roy's work will stem criticism of this design, and set the record straight at last.

BASICALLY SAME AS ORIGINAL MONSTER BUT IMPRESSION OF COMPOSITE HEAD WOULD BE HELPED BY SEPARATE PIECE FOR FOREHEAD — SEPARATE EARS & NOSE IN SLIGHTLY DIFFERENT COLOURED PLASTIC - DEFINITE STITCH MARKS — FOREHEAD RECEDING — AND POORLY GROWING HAIR — ELECTRODES ABOVE EAR — THIS CAN BE PUT ANYWHERE WITHOUT DIFFICULTY.

> **Elizabeth Ashton:**
> **He used to keep these things to himself, except once or twice when he was really annoyed that they hadn't selected what he thought was a good idea. Roy bottled it all up you see. That's what he was like when he was annoyed. He wouldn't say anything. He never moaned about anyone to me.**

The Gorgon

The Gorgon
Production Details: Released October 18, 1964 (UK), February 17, 1965 (US); 83 Minutes (UK); Eastmancolor; 7497 Feet; A Hammer Film Production; A BLC Release (UK), A Columbia Release (US); Filmed at Bray Studios; Director: Terence Fisher; Producer: Anthony Nelson Keys; Screenplay: John Gilling, John Elder ; Music: James Bernard; Music Supervisor: Marcus Dods; Director of Photography: Michael Reed; Supervising Editor: James Needs; Production Manager: Don Weeks; Sound Recordist: Ken Rawkins; Camera: Cece Cooney; Continuity: Pauline Harlow; Wardrobe: Molly Arbuthnot and Rosemary Burrows ; Hairdresser: Fieda Steiger; Make-Up: Roy Ashton; Art Director: Don Mingaye; Production Design: Bernard Robinson; Assistant Director: Bert Batt; Special Effects: Syd Pearson; UK Certificate: X.

Cast List: Peter Cushing (Dr. Namaroff), Christopher Lee (Professor Meister), Barbara Shelley (Carla), Richard Pasco (Paul), Michael Goodliffe (Professor Heitz), Patrick Troughton (Kanof), Prudence Hyman (The Gorgon)

> **Oddly enough I found my first female subject, Barbara Shelley, to be far less squeamish than most male actors at being made to appear hideous!**

Megaera is the sister of Stheno, Euryale and Medusa from the legends of ancient Greece. Megaera has survived the ages in transcendent spirit form, occasionally inhabiting the body of a beautiful young women. Like many of these supernatural creatures she takes her actual form to feed under the influence of the full-moon. In this case, Megaera's long tresses become living serpents, her skin takes on the texture of a snake. Of course in Grecian myth anyone falling directly under her gaze is turned into stone. But in the script, this petrification is because of the bites of her snake filled hair.

According to the Hammer Publicity Department, *The Gorgon* is 'a living horror.' Roy Ashton would have agreed with this assessment, but for different reasons. For the first time Roy Ashton's conception of a monster would be rejected by the Hammer management. Barbara Shelley would share the Jekyll and Hyde role with another actress, Prudence Hyman. Francis Wyndham, a Sunday Times Magazine reporter, was allowed access to Bray Studios during production. Wyndham's article *The Sub Cinema* provides an intriguing glimpse of the making of *The Gorgon*:

At Bray Studios, the Hammer Horror Factory, where the latest specimen, The Gorgon was being made, the atmosphere was strikingly cosy: here film-making is a domestic affair, with family jokes and even a suggestion of nursery games. The producer, Anthony Nelson Keys (son of Butch Keys, the comedian), has a clown's kind rubbery face: this is his first solo production although as general manager of Bray Studios he has been involved in all the others. "The Gorgon is a bit subtler than the usual horror film" he pointed out, "because there isn't any blood. There's stone instead! We do have a lot of fun making these films but we don't do them with our tongue in our cheek: we take them seriously. It's got to be convincing when Professor Heitz is turned to stone. The set depicted the entrance hall of Castle Borski, home of the dreaded Gorgon, Megaera. Murky mirrors, broken statues,

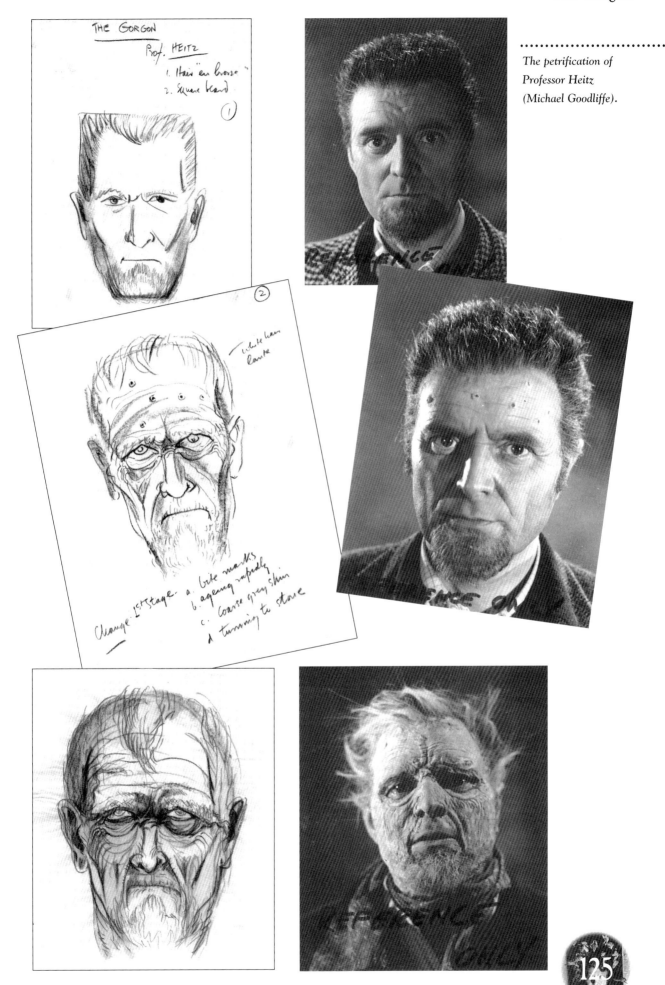

The petrification of
Professor Heitz
(Michael Goodliffe).

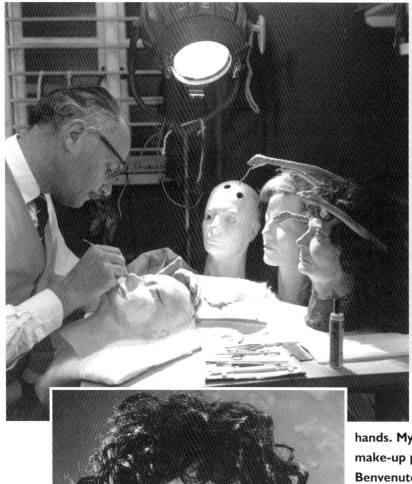

dusty tapestry, shattered stained glass, tattered flags, antlers and a tilted chandelier... all bathed in a green light, for green is the classic shade of horror and Hammer Films take pride in the quality of their colour. Cobwebs, spun from rubber solution, had been sprayed over the furniture. The Gorgon herself, incarnated by the actress Prudence Hyman, sat knitting in a deck chair, her face covered in hideous scales. She wore a dressing gown, beneath which her winkle pickers looked incongruously smart. Her wig, a triumph for 'special effects' with its tangle of serpents whose heads rear up, eyes light up and tongues protrude, was still in the charge of the make-up man, Roy Ashton.

"The design for *The Gorgon* was really taken out of my hands. My idea was to base the snake make-up partly on the celebrated Benvenuto Cellini idea of the severed head. In this marvellous sculpture of a warrior holding the severed head of the Medusa the snakes were in small clusters rather than two or three big serpents as in the film. Really, each lock of hair should be a serpent. That would have been my approach to it. I considered a writhing effect could have been achieved by making vipers from coloured wood attached to leather strips. These are sometimes available as children's toys and can look most realistic with the proper lighting. I thought that if they went about it that way, they could have the appearance of a constant sinuous movement. But the management didn't agree with me so they gave it to what then became established as a special effects department. They made snakes which were activated by remote control by a series of long cables attached to cams and a crank that wound these things up. That really wasn't to my taste. I felt that the snakes were too big and static. As far as regarding my work on *The Gorgon* as a failure I suppose it could be seen as a failure to satisfy the management. But I didn't agree with the exposition of *The Gorgon*, she should have been a mass of writhing serpents."

Top:
Syd Pearson works on special effects.

Above:
Prudence Hyman's make-up test.

Barbara Shelley:

"I knew that Roy was unhappy with *The Gorgon*, and I never ever thought of it as Roy's mistake, ever! Because, somehow to me doing that film Roy was so distant – probably mentally as well as physically. Because when the Gorgon rig was actually being used, there was Prudence walking around with this crowd of people behind her, puffing air into these rubber snakes. To actually photograph that with any degree of reality it would have had to be very much more darkly lit. The solution was that the Gorgon should have been more of a suggestion. Perhaps if they had shown her from behind, or maybe an approaching shadow, a reaction shot and then a face turn, and it was a hideous face covered in snakes and then gone. That would have more in keeping with Roy's ideas. I lost any fear of snakes when I was very young, and just started modeling. I was asked to handle a Boa Constrictor at a photo-shoot at the zoo. I thought that it was going to be cold and slimy, because they sliver like worms, but it was warm, and soft, a lovely feeling, a bit like nursing a cat. Had I been given my famous crown of real snakes and been allowed to play both Carla and Megaera in *The Gorgon*, I am sure that real snakes would have been far more acceptable."

Christopher Lee:

"This of course was the least effective of the make-ups. Special effects were so much in their infancy in those days. Each snake was manipulated individually with wires, it was virtually impossible. Think of what you could do today with computers and opticals. It could be fantastic. But these snakes were rigid and consequently, you shouldn't really have a wig. The whole thing should be writhing. Again I don't think either Roy or Syd Pearson were given enough time to work on it."

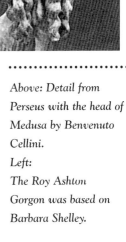

Above: *Detail from Perseus with the head of Medusa by Benvenuto Cellini.*
Left:
The Roy Ashton Gorgon was based on Barbara Shelley.

Elizabeth Ashton:

"Roy was very annoyed about what happened on *The Gorgon*. But it was typical of

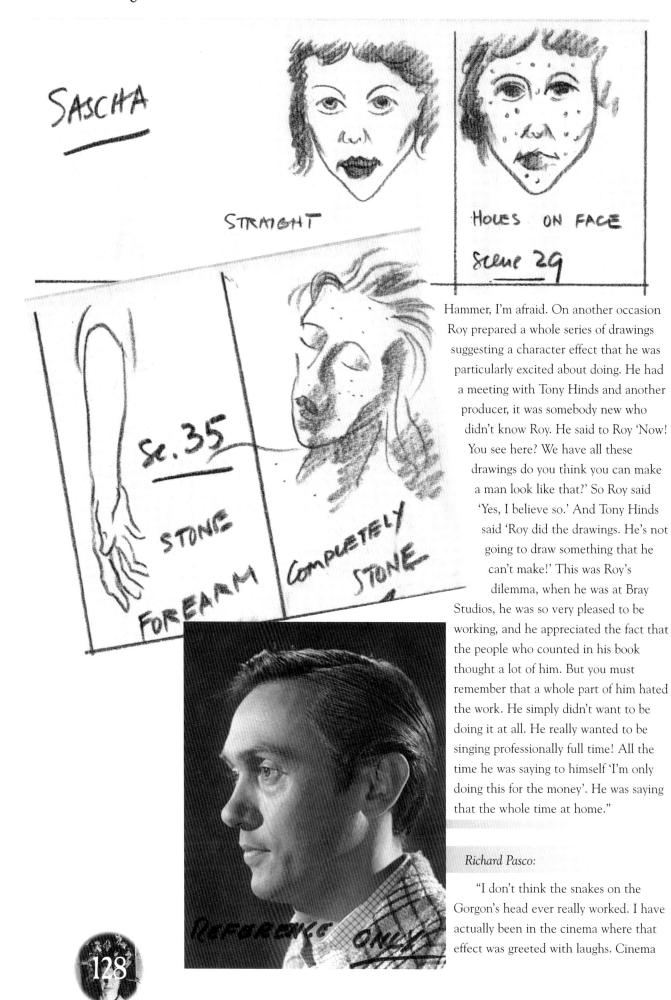

SASCHA

STRAIGHT

HOLES ON FACE

Scene 29

Sc. 35

STONE FOREARM

COMPLETELY STONE

REFERENCE ONLY

Hammer, I'm afraid. On another occasion Roy prepared a whole series of drawings suggesting a character effect that he was particularly excited about doing. He had a meeting with Tony Hinds and another producer, it was somebody new who didn't know Roy. He said to Roy 'Now! You see here? We have all these drawings do you think you can make a man look like that?' So Roy said 'Yes, I believe so.' And Tony Hinds said 'Roy did the drawings. He's not going to draw something that he can't make!' This was Roy's dilemma, when he was at Bray Studios, he was so very pleased to be working, and he appreciated the fact that the people who counted in his book thought a lot of him. But you must remember that a whole part of him hated the work. He simply didn't want to be doing it at all. He really wanted to be singing professionally full time! All the time he was saying to himself 'I'm only doing this for the money'. He was saying that the whole time at home."

Richard Pasco:

"I don't think the snakes on the Gorgon's head ever really worked. I have actually been in the cinema where that effect was greeted with laughs. Cinema

128

audiences are quite sophisticated now, even the youngest ones, because they are used to such incredible computer effects. When you see something like that, which really doesn't work, everything else is ruined and I can quite understand Roy's position. He obviously went into quite a lot of detail. I can only remember Roy as being a delightful man, highly professional, co-operative, kind and considerate. I couldn't think of a nicer man to be made-up by at six o'clock in the morning. I was actually a victim of the Gorgon. I was partially turned to stone and I had to lay down and go to bed. I don't know what happened there. I suppose I got better."

"I had made plaster casts of the various character's heads and I then coloured the casts as if they were made out of stone. The producers were in considerable difficulties about Sasha, a girl who had to turn into stone at the beginning of the film. This was to have been a full-length shot of her body. Skin doesn't represent much difficulty in creating a petrified effect, it was her hair that was going to be a problem 'Well' they said: 'surely its easy enough, all you have to do is dip the wig into plaster and it will solidify.' 'Yes', I said, 'and what do I send back to the wigmakers? You can't knock a plaster coated wig back into shape with a sledge-hammer and return it to the shop in tiny pieces.' 'Alright' they said. 'Can you help us here?' I gave the problem careful consideration and made a lady's wig out of plasticine and coloured it to resemble stone. It weighed a ton but, the final result was a quite good effect and saved Hammer the cost of replacing a ruined wig which was then in the region of £60."

The Gorgon

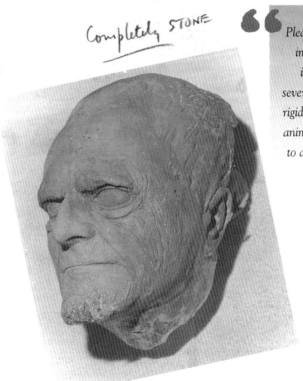

The GORGON

Prof. HEITZ

final stage 5

Completely STONE

Although Roy didn't get his way with the Gorgon's writhing tresses, the rest of his work on this film is exemplary. The sequences where the actors are turned to stone are compelling, and the Gorgon's face (if you block off the rubber snakes) is literally petrifying. Roy's designs, reproduced here, demonstrate his usual attention to detail, and this work is considered by some to be the redeeming characteristic of the film. Film historian, Robert Murphy writes:

> "The woebegone appearance of the Gorgon herself is disappointing, but the turning to stone sequences - which rely as much on the performances of Michael Goodliffe and Richard Pasco as on make-up, are very effective."

Roy embraced the romantic concepts central to the legend of The Gorgon. He perceived a strange wonderfulness in the distortion of conventional beauty. Roy would have wholly agreed with Percy Bysshe Shelley's assessment of the painting of The Medusa in the Uffizi Gallery:

> *Pleasure and pain are combined in one single impression. the very objects which should induce a shudder – the livid face of the severed head, the squirming mass of vipers, the rigidity of death, the sinister light, the repulsive animals, the lizard, the bat – all these give rise to a new sense of beauty, a beauty imperilled and contaminated – a new thrill!*

She

She
Production Details: Released April 18, 1965 (UK), September 1, 1965 (US); 104 Minutes; Metrocolor; 9324 Feet; A Hammer 7 Arts Production; An MGM Release; Filmed at Elstree Studios and on location in Israel; Director: Robert Day; Producer: Michael Carreras; Associate Producer: Aida Young; Screen Play: David T. Chantler; Music: James Bernard; Music Supervisor: Philip Martell; Director of Photography: Harry Waxman; Editor: James Needs and Eric Boyd-Perkins; Production Manager: Ri L.M. Davidson; Sound Recordist: Claude Hitchcock; Camera: Ernest Day; Continuity: Eileen Head; Wardrobe: Jackie Cummins; Hairdresser: Eileen Warwick; Make-Up: John O'Gorman; Special Make-Up Effects: Roy Ashton; Transformation Sequence: Roy Ashton; Art Director: Robert Jones; Production Design: Bernard Robinson; Assistant Director: Bruce Sharman; Special Effects: George Blackwell and Bowie Films Ltd.; UK Certificate: X.

Cast List: Ursula Andress (Ayesha), Peter Cushing (Major Holly), Bernard Cribbins (Job), John Richardson (Leo), Christopher Lee (Billali), Rosenda Monteros (Ustane), Andre Morrell (Haumeid)

"When I was asked to supervise the transformation sequence in *She*, Ursula Andress asked the producer 'Roy Ashton? Who's he?' and was told 'Oh, he's a special man: he specializes in curious effects.' I don't mind that designation. There's great pleasure in working with a female actress doing a nice slick job and making her look lovely. Great satisfaction in that. But it's not as exacting or taxing a matter as dreaming up some very unusual character with a good beard and bags under the eyes and all the rest of it. Yet despite all my preparatory work it was an unnerving experience to start my day by taking such a young and attractive woman and transforming her as she slept, into an ancient, gibbering crone!"

She

The charismatic title of H. Rider Haggard's story celebrates Ayesha, the beautiful and terrible: She who must be obeyed! In the Hammer version of this much filmed 1887 novel, Ayesha has been worshipped by generations of slaves as a Goddess-Queen, the absolute ruler of a city state preserved in the desert for 2,000 years. She has achieved immortality by bathing in the ice blue flames of a mystic fire, but Ayesha has experienced several lifetimes of loneliness, waiting for the reincarnation of her lover, Killikrates. In a fit of jealous rage, Ayesha had him put to death millennia before and is forced to mourn over his mummified remains. At the dawn of the 20th century, She receives reports that her beloved has returned. Killikrates has been reborn as the British adventurer Leo Vincey, who had been left behind in Egypt after the First World War. Ayesha has him kidnapped and transported to her city. After failing to convince Leo of his destiny to rule as a god by her side, she returns to the magic fire to prove he has nothing to fear from the ritual. However, a second visit to the flames proves fatal and Ayesha assumes the hideous appearance of her true age. Ayesha's transformation is the climax of the film and is described in detail in Haggard's novel:

"Smaller and smaller she grew; her skin changed colour, and in place of the perfect whiteness of its lustre it turned dirty brown and yellow, like an old piece of withered parchment. She felt at her head: the delicate hand was nothing but a claw now, a human talon resembling that of a badly preserved Egyptian mummy. Then she seemed to understand what kind of change was passing over her, and she shrieked – ah she shrieked! – Ayesha rolled upon the floor and shrieked. Smaller she grew and smaller yet, till she was no larger than a monkey. Now the skin had puckered into a million wrinkles, and on her shapeless face was the stamp of unutterable age. I never saw anything like it; nobody saw anything to equal the infinite age which was graven on that fearful countenance, no bigger now than that of a two months' old child, though the skull retained its same size; and let all men pray that they never shall, if they wish to keep their reason. At last she lay still, or only moving feebly. She, who but two minutes gone had gazed upon us – the

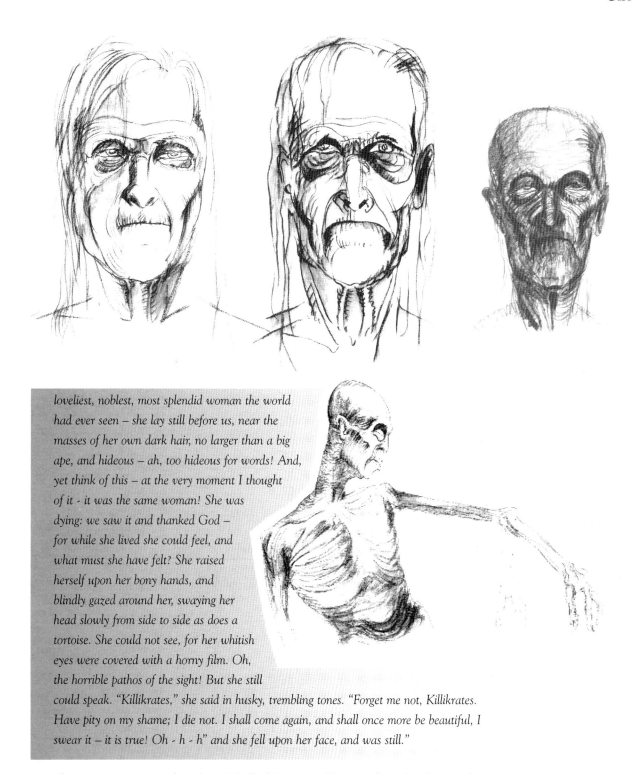

loveliest, noblest, most splendid woman the world had ever seen – she lay still before us, near the masses of her own dark hair, no larger than a big ape, and hideous – ah, too hideous for words! And, yet think of this – at the very moment I thought of it - it was the same woman! She was dying: we saw it and thanked God – for while she lived she could feel, and what must she have felt? She raised herself upon her bony hands, and blindly gazed around her, swaying her head slowly from side to side as does a tortoise. She could not see, for her whitish eyes were covered with a horny film. Oh, the horrible pathos of the sight! But she still could speak. "Killikrates," she said in husky, trembling tones. "Forget me not, Killikrates. Have pity on my shame; I die not. I shall come again, and shall once more be beautiful, I swear it – it is true! Oh - h - h" and she fell upon her face, and was still."

She was a pet project of producer Michael Carreras: "Casting the title role was of course, our biggest problem. As soon as we saw Ursula Andress walk out of the sea in *Dr. No* we knew there was only one woman to play Haggard's Queen. We had to wait two years before she was free of other commitments, but it was worth it." Co-starring with Frank Sinatra and his 'rat-pack' in *4 For Texas (1963)* and Elvis in *Fun in Acapulco (1963)* the Hammer publicity machine described the Swiss born actress as: 'THE MOST BEAUTIFUL WOMAN IN THE WORLD'. The press book states: "People talk about Ursula Andress as though she invented sex. You can't blame them. Her assets are impressive. Honey blonde hair, light brown eyes with flecks of yellow in them, a pouting mouth and a perfect figure." The challenge for the make-up artist was

STAGE 2

PATCHES OF GRANULATED TISSUE - DISCOLOURED GREY & PINK . HAIR
BECOMING PATCHY IN COLOUR - BROWNS - ODD PATCHES OF GREY

STAGE 3   MOUTH BEGINNING TO DROOP
PATCHY SKIN - REDNESS ALMOST GONE - EYES BAGGING - LARGE
CREASES - NECK CREASES APPEARING - HAIR ALMOST GREY. LANK & PATCHY

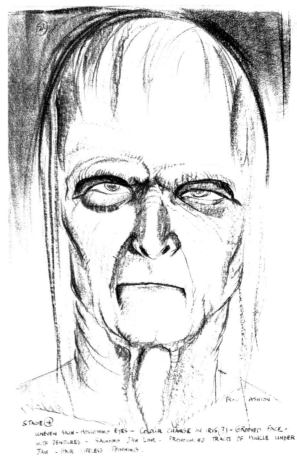

STAGE 4
UNEVEN SKIN - HOLLOWING EYES - COLOUR CHANGE IN IRIS(?) - GROOVED FACE -
WITH DENTURES - SAGGING JAW LINE - PRONOUNCED TRACTS OF MUSCLE UNDER
JAW - HAIR LIFELESS THINNING .

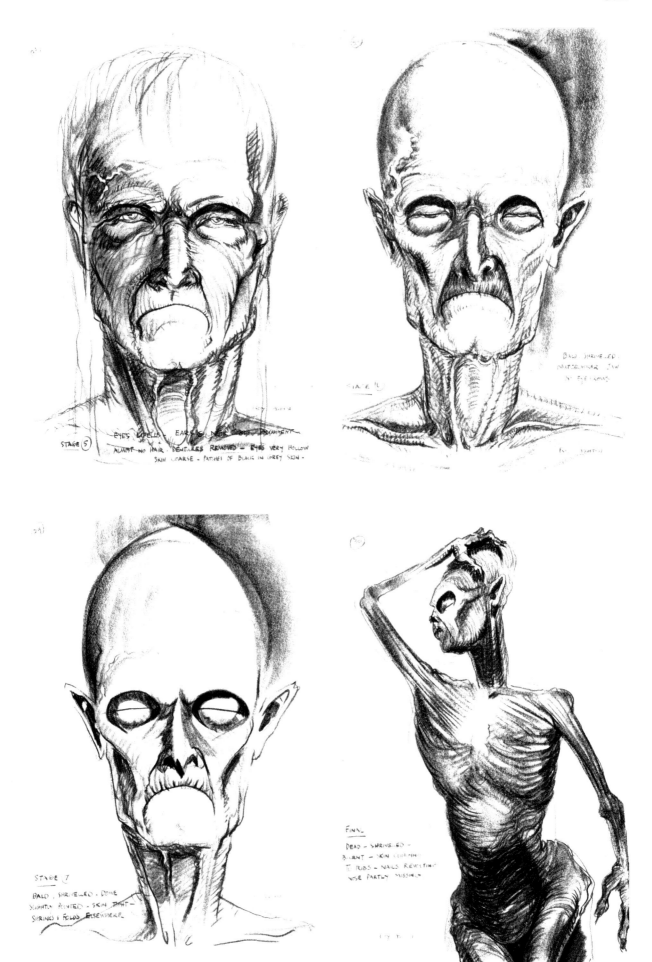

STAGE (5) EYES EYELIDS - EARS NECK LOBES PROMINENT -
ALMOST NO HAIR - DENTURES REMOVED - EYES VERY HOLLOW
SKIN COARSE - PATCHES OF BLACK IN GREY SKIN -

STAGE 6
BALD SHRIVELED
NEITHER NOSE JAW
NO EYEBROWS

STAGE 7
BALD - SHRIVELED - DOME
SLIGHTLY POINTED - SKIN TIGHT -
SHRINKS & FOLDS ELSEWHERE -

FINAL
DEAD - SHRIVELED -
BURNT - SKIN CURLING -
TO RIBS - NAILS REVOLTING
NOSE PARTLY MISSING -

to both glamourise Ursula's natural assets and provide the horrific flip-side by transforming her into a decomposing monster. Unbelievable as this may seem considering his track record at Hammer, Roy Ashton was not chosen to supervise make-up on this film.

Elizabeth Ashton:

"The first time Roy heard about *She* was when the production was already under way. I remember the producers ringing him up in a panic. Roy placed his hand over the receiver and said 'Guess what? They brought someone else in to do the make-up and they can't do the transformation scene! Why didn't they give me the whole job to begin with?' That really annoyed Roy, being passed over, then having to pull someone else's irons out of the fire. But the final insult was doing all that work then not getting any screen credit for designing and executing the highlight of the picture."

*Aida Young
(Associate Producer):*

"It wasn't me who called Roy Ashton in. It must have been Michael Carreras. I knew nothing about it. But I remember

how he aged Ursula Andress. That took us all day to shoot. We put aside a Saturday, so
that we could concentrate on it. We called in only the people who needed to be
involved with the ageing. Today, of course, her face would get old on a computer. It
could be done in twenty minutes. Roy was so innovative and so technically excellent.

It was very traumatic for Ursula. She was looking in the make-up mirror, watching
herself get older, and she couldn't stand it. She was in floods of tears. She was such a
beautiful, young girl, and then she looked older. I mean it: floods of tears. I was called
to the make-up room to pacify her, get her to stop crying and get on with it. Ursula
wanted to do the scene, but she really hadn't realised what it would be like watching

herself get older. The second shot of her ageing was what upset her. The later stages were rather grotesque, and she didn't mind those. But that second stage was so realistic, so true to life, she couldn't take it."

The Roy Ashton collection includes detailed notes concerning how the transformation of Ayesha was to be achieved. This part of the collection is of significant interest, as it is a detailed and complete record of Roy's work on a complex

transformation. We get a feel for how Roy's creative thoughts developed, and for his enthusiasm to succeed convincingly.

The following is taken from those various notes which Roy Ashton made to accompany his drawings. These notes and production designs indicate that Roy intended to use two other actresses in addition to Ursula Andress:

The first few stages are the only ones in which Ursula Andress should be used, because the prosthetic appliances will increase some of the dimensions of the human body. Since the fundamental process involves various

representations of shrinkage, emaciation, withering, shriveling, and destruction, prosthetics may only be applied to produce an alteration of skin texture, changes in the granulation of the bone structure, tissue disintegration and the thinning in texture and eventual loss of hair. The initial stages are indicated by a change of colouring on the face and body. When flesh is consumed by fire the colours intensify. Strange reds and blacks are produced beneath the skin until the body is roasted and scorched. These gradations in colour should be fully explored before Ayesha's final death. The ageing process in the face and hands of the original artist are enhanced. The grey granulation of her skin is flecked with pink. Her hair is singed at the ends. First effects are introduced deepening the eye sockets, creating crows feet and bags under the orbits, as the skin starts to sag and lose its elasticity. The eyes themselves could be further changed by 'watery' contact lenses such as the one's I used in *The Man Who Could Cheat Death*. Towards the end of the first stage, Ayesha's skin becomes increasingly patchy in colour and texture. Her blood and vascular systems become more visually pronounced almost with the effort of pumping her coagulating life blood around her carcass. At the same time, her hair is being lost and the arms are becoming distressed. Wrinkles cover all areas of exposed flesh. After the first few changes

the original artist should not be used, but replaced by a woman of similar bone structure and less massively built. The ageing effects should be transferred progressively from one to the other. However, the first substitute artist for close shots of the face should be smaller in stature and much older than Ursula Andress. The hair piece is thinner and whatever natural signs of ageing are already evident should be emphasized. With the introduction of a second substitute artist for full body shots: the collapse of the vascular system is announced along with the prominent appearance of the sternum and mastoid structures. The wrinkled skin cells become hard and heavy. Several overlapping plate-like clusters develop. The third substitute artist: assists the transfer from the second substitute artist to animated sculpture. This artist is virtually hairless with only a handful of long wispy strands remaining. The final shriveled and dying immovable body, should be modeled on a skeleton of the appropriate size matching the original actress. I will increase all previous suggestions of decomposition to resemble a reptilian being. The exact textures can then be perfectly reproduced or made exactly to the producer's wishes. Destruction is by fire. In the script, there is no mention made of disease. However, I feel that if the shock effect of this scene is to be increased this should be conveyed by some indication of abnormal physical and mental traits. The horror of Ayesha's situation transformed from a glamorous young woman into a 2,000 year old hag can be suggested through a host of deformities a la 'Dorian Grey'. Some alternative suggestions for the final appearance of She are given emphasizing this idea.

The final stage of the sequence was to incorporate an animated sculpture improving on 'the corpse' Roy had already produced for *Paranoiac*. Roy's conception well exceeded the effects normally used in Hammer films. Although *She* remains an undoubted highlight in Roy Ashton's career, one must regret the loss of yet another opportunity for Roy to excel at his craft. At least based on the fragments that survive on paper we may indulge our imaginations and wonder what this sequence could have become on celluloid if Roy had been given the appropriate resources and support his talent deserved? We can only imagine Roy's disappointment when he discovered that he only had the one day to actualize the entire transformation effect.

Aida Young:
"When people plan a sequence by storyboard, they can get carried away... very ambitious. When the time comes to shoot it, you have a very limited time to do it, certainly at Hammer. Then, something goes by the board!"

The Plague Of The Zombies

The Plague Of The Zombies Production Details: Released January 9, 1966 (UK), January 12, 1966 (US); 90 Minutes; Technicolor; A Hammer - 7 Arts Film Production; A Associated British Warner Pathé Release (UK), 20th Century Fox Release (US); Filmed at Bray Studios; Director: John Gilling; Executive Producer: Anthony Hinds; Producer: Anthony Nelson-Keys; Screenplay: John Elder, Peter Bryan; Music: James Bernard; Music Supervisor: Philip Martell; Director of Photography: Arthur Grant; Supervising Editor: James Needs; Editor: Chris Barnes; Production Manager: George Fowler; Sound Recordist: Ken Rawkins; Camera: Moray Grant; Continuity: Lorna Selwyn; Wardrobe: Rosemary Burrows; Hairdresser: Frieda Steiger; Make-Up: Roy Ashton; Art Director: Don Mingaye; Production Design: Bernard Robinson; Assistant Director: Bert Batt, Martyn Green; Special Effects: Bowie Films Ltd.; UK Certificate: X.

Cast List: André Morell (Sir James Forbes), Diane Clare (Syvia Forbes), Brook Williams (Dr. Peter Thompson), Jacqueline Pearce (Alice Thompson), John Carson (Squire Hamilton), Alex Davion (Denver), Michael Ripper (Sergeant Swift), Del Watson, Peter Diamond (Zombies)

> " Creating an army of zombies and the ritual paraphenalia of voodoo that goes with it was not easy. I had to research this one, as I knew little about it. It turned out to be rather interesting. "

The Plague of the Zombies

The films released by Hammer in 1966 represent an an extremely fertile period. Made back to back, the "Cornish" pictures, as they became known, consisted of *Plague of the Zombies* and *The Reptile*. These two films are notable for two outstanding reasons: The introduction of Jacqueline Pearce, who has been described as the most sensual of Hammer heroines, and the creation of two of Roy Ashton's best ever monsters. In *Plague of the Zombies*, Hammer transferred Voodoo from the Caribbean to the England of 1905. Well versed in occult lore, Squire Hamilton slays and reanimates the bodies of Cornish villagers to work in his tin mine. Only the local doctor Peter Thompson and his mentor, Sir James Forbes dare investigate the mysterious deaths.

According to the Voodoo legends of Haiti, a Zombie is a harmless creature. In spiritual terms it is an empty body. The consciousness that once belonged to the cadaver is now possessed by Loa: the Voodoo deities brought forth into the mortal realm by the beating of drums, dancing bodies and blood sacrifice. Once the Loa remove a human soul, the Zombie will enter a death - like state and have no will of its own. After a period resting in its grave, the Zombie is resurrected to toil as a slave, their actions controlled by an evil sorcerer or Bokor.

Jackie Pearce – The most sensual of Hammer heroines.

Rotting skins can be suggested through a mixture of rubber and paper, then a careful application of cosmetics. By crumpling up tissue paper, colouring it with Fuller's earth and then covering it with liquid latex, one can create a very effective specimen. Areas on the face on which to demonstrate crumbling scabs or splitting skins include: the forehead, the bridge of the nose, or chin as natural starting points. I would suggest building up an excess of material and then shred the latex slightly by gentle tearing. The final touch is a pair of contact lenses for those bleached out eyes. For *The Plague of the Zombies* I designed several sets of contact lenses with reverse tone values, white pupils with black backgrounds, or in some cases plain white lenses with pin sized appertures to enable the performer to see. I used to put the contact lenses in the artists' eyes myself. There were no problems with this make-up, patience and care in its application is the essential factor. As for design I used a handful of my favourite medical text books and a generous helping of imagination.

A make-up test on a zombie (Ben Aris).

Jacqueline Pearce:

"Roy was a total professional who took it all very seriously. He gave a great deal of thought to the design and application of the make-up and was of course very much an artist in his own field. We went in one at a time to make-up. There was a large cast needing special make-up, especially in the dream sequence. But I don't have any memories of 30 people crowding into makeup to be turned into a crowd of Zombies. We were made up very efficiently for what we had to do and then Roy moved on to whoever needed his attention next. As far as I can remember the Zombie make-up was quite elaborate on some people. My make-up was really just ordinary cosmetics but layered in different shades of grey. So it wasn't too horrendous. The other Zombies were wearing contact lenses, and this didn't seem to bother them. You couldn't have got me to do it for love nor money! It was a very light-hearted shoot. I think the actors fell about with laughter quite frequently. Probably, on more than one occasion the powers that be told us that we had to take it more seriously. But one does feel silly standing around in a graveyard at 3 o'clock on a Wednesday afternoon made-up as a Zombie."

Roy applies blood to a discreetly covered Jacqueline Pearce

The main artist, Jacqueline Pearce, was supposed to lie in a coffin in a grave in that film, but she was so claustrophobic, that when the time arrived she flatly refused. It was only when the first assistant director Bert Batt offered to lie beneath her that she agreed to enter the grave. He talked to her all the time to keep her calm.

Jacqueline Pearce:

"I absolutely adored Bert Batt. He was very kind and kept the whole show together. I enjoyed making it because I enjoyed the people I was working with – particularly the crew. I was a beginner and they were very kind to me and showed me the ropes. Bray Studio was such a lovely studio to work in. It was so homely. There was a wonderful cook there who did devastating treacle sponge puddings. So I got rather fat but it was great fun.

I do remember that I had to have my head chopped off in this scene and a replica head had to be made. Roy put Plaster of Paris all over my face. Only the nostrils were left so that I could breathe. I was very claustrophobic in those days and I remember it had to be left on for 30 minutes to set properly. On the 29th minute I said: 'I can't take any more of this.' I began to thrash about and it all had to be ripped off and started again. It was a nightmare. I don't think it was something that anybody would want to go through voluntarily. Roy was very patient with me. I

Top: Concept watercolours of Denver's mask and the actual mask in place on actor Alex Davion.

Below right: Watercolour of Hamilton's mask

Below left: Jackie Pearce feeling silly at three o'clock on a Wednesday afternoon!

Mask for DENVER in "Plague of the Zombies"
Roy ASHTON

Voodoo Mask for HAMILTON in "Plague of the Zombies"
Roy ASHTON

had a cup of tea to relax. I noticed that Roy had drawings and other works in various stages of development. As he re-applied the plaster to my face, Roy chatted about how he would achieve some of the effects he was after. I didn't regard this as unusual. I suppose at that age, because I was very young and just starting out, I accepted that this was his world and that's how he functioned within it. When I saw my head on the shelf in the make-up room the next morning, that was altogether another experience. I think that if Roy's make-up defined what Zombies ought to look like in that film, then he had the prototype in me darling. I'm not an early morning lady!"

Above:
Jackie Pearce examines her plaster cast head, while in costume for The Reptile.

Left:Jackie gets swept off her feet by a young, attractive zombie (Ben Aris).

As it hardens plaster both contracts and generates a great deal of heat. Therefore I have never been completely surprised when an artist reacts against a cast being made. After all they are required to breathe through straws up their nostrils whilst deprived of almost all of their natural senses... Do you know that I have never actually seen *The Plague Of The Zombies*? We were always so busy preparing for the next production that we had barely time to see the day's rushes.

The concept of a zombie which Roy created for this film, was wholly original. The gaunt, putrified visage with its blanked out eyes and small black pupils shambles into close-up, and snaps open its jaw, revealing rancid gums and teeth. This Ashton creation made such a profound impact on the horror cinema, that no conception of a zombie has since been able to move entirely away from it. Roy had created an icon!

Rosemary Burrows (Wardrobe):

"Roy's ideas for the zombies were brilliant. But we couldn't put them in proper clothes, could we? We brought in loads of sacking, and it was all hands to the sewing machines! I can't remember how many sack cloth outfits we knocked up, but it was a big operation. There was more than thirty outfits. We needed them all at once for the finale, when the mine burns down."

The Plague of the Zombies

While the Zombie creation demands our attention, it is important to notice the efforts Roy put into the voodoo masks. These masks were based upon Roy's own researches into voodoo tradition, and his original watercolour ideas are presented here for the first time.

Above: The mask in place on John Carson (Hamilton), including Roy's bootlaces.

The voodoo masks were the result of both documentation and imagination. I scratched my head a good deal about ideas for that one, investigating upon voodoo ceremonies on the Caribbean Islands. For instance, there was a certain symbolism in the letters 'BS' which were appearing on the forehead: an abbreviation of 'Baron Samedi', a colourful story in itself... I was very puzzled as well about choosing the substance to make it. After pondering on the matter I went home, where I unearthed an old polishing cloth that I had been using on the motor car for years and which by that time looked pretty disgusting. I cut the voodoo mask out of it. While the little leather thongs on it were actually my own boot laces. You know I also created one with horns for the film, inspired by some of the things used by South African tribes. It looked odd and queer and gave some sort of remote suggestion... When Tony Keys saw both of them, he said: 'Yes, that is great!'. As soon as they come to a decision like that, it does save me a lot of worrying! I couldn't have stood another 'song and dance' about masks, like we had on Phantom!

The Reptile

The Reptile
Production Details: Released March 6, 1966 (UK), April 6, 1966 (US); 91 Minutes; Technicolor; A Hammer - 7 Arts Film Production; A Warner Pathe Release (UK), 20th Century Fox Release (US); Filmed at Bray Studios; Director: John Gilling; Executive Producer: Anthony Hinds; Producer: Anthony Nelson-Keys; Screenplay: John Elder; Music: Don Banks; Music Supervisor: Philip Martell; Director of Photography: Arthur Grant; Supervising Editor: James Needs; Editor: Roy Hyde; Production Manager: George Fowler; Sound Recordist: Bill Buckley; Camera: Moray Grant; Continuity: Lorna Selwyn; Wardrobe: Rosemary Burrows; Hairdresser: Frieda Steiger; Make-Up: Roy Ashton; Art Director: Don Mingaye; Production Design: Bernard Robinson; Assistant Director: Bill Cartlidge; Special Effects: Bowie Films Ltd.; UK Certificate: X.

Cast List: Noel Willman (Dr. Franklyn), Jennifer Daniel (Valerie Spalding), Ray Barrett (Harry Spalding), Jacqueline Pearce (Anna), Michael Ripper (Tom Bailey), John Laurie (Mad Peter), Marne Maitland (Malay), David Baron (Charles Spaulding), Charles Lloyd Pack (Vicar), Harold Goldblatt (Solicitor), George Woodbridge (Old Garnsey)

“ *The Reptile* certainly gave me some problems. The young lady concerned – Jackie Pearce suffered from claustrophobia – and was inclined to rip off all the make-up. I had a real struggle to get it on. I even had to make some separate eyepieces which I clamped on just before each take – quite a business! ”

The Reptile

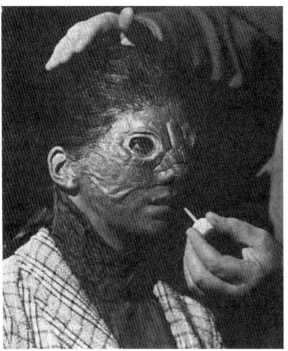

Although never released on the same cinema bill, *The Reptile* is widely regarded as a companion piece to *The Plague Of The Zombies*. The film is set in the fictitious village of Clagmoor, Cornwall in 1902. The death of Charles Spalding brings his brother Harry and wife Valerie to investigate. The Spaldings are aided by the landlord of the local pub, Tom Bailey, in solving the mystery. This is Hammer stalwart, Michael Ripper's meatiest role and is reminiscent of the nemesis of evil frequently played by Peter Cushing. Despite *The Reptile* being labelled as a 'Cornish Picture' the motivating force of the vengeful serpent woman brings the

Above:
Roy applies creative touches to The Reptile

Left:
Ashton explores anatomical detail for the Serpent Woman

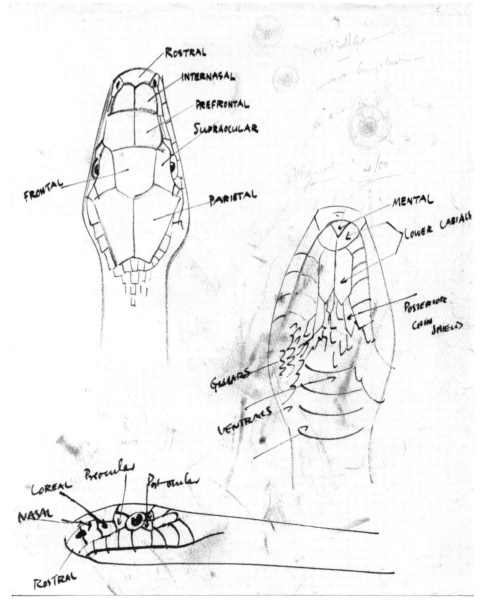

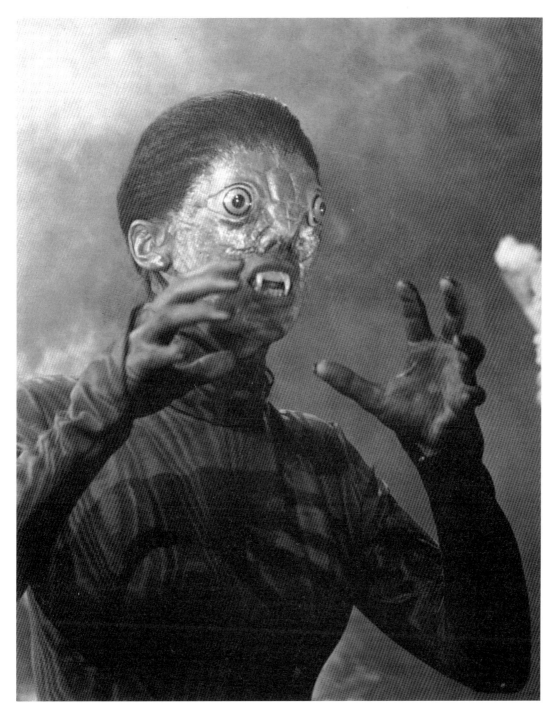

film closer to the themes explored earlier in *The Gorgon*. Just as the unwitting female carrier of the spirit of Megaera is a prisoner of Dr Namaroff, in *The Reptile*, Anna is likewise imprisoned by her father, Dr Franklyn. Anna is also unaware that she is possessed by a malignant supernatural force. As revenge against her father's interference in their occult practices, the Ourang Sancto – the Snake people of Borneo, initiate Anna into their cult. Consequently, the quiet of rural England is disturbed by Anna, who transforms into a deadly human serpent.

A lot of research went into the appearance of the Reptile. Again I consulted anatomical authorities, drew snakes many times and constructed a model adapting the plate-like build-up of reptilian scales to the bones of the human head. There is a clear similarity of the human head to the structure of a snake's skull.

The Reptile

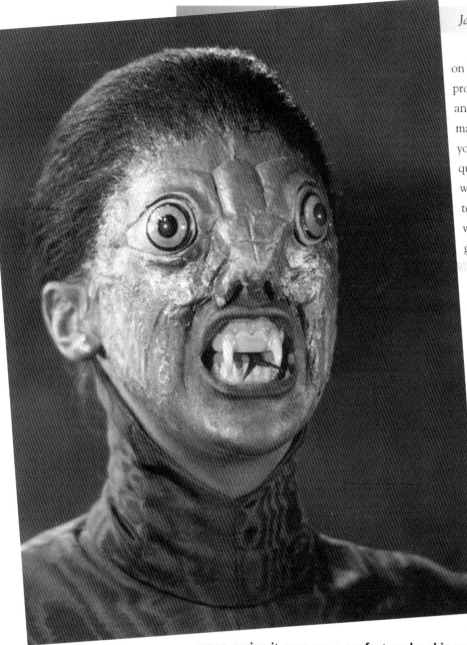

One cannot gaze upon that fearsome countenance without a shudder...

Jacqueline Pearce

"Before we finished shooting on *The Plague Of The Zombies* the producer called me into his office and said: "You've got a marvellous face for films, I'd like you to play the Reptile." I never quite understood that! There were quite elaborate make-up tests, so that Roy knew what we were going to do long before we got on the floor of the studio."

I made the basic mask from laminated paper to be built around the head of the artist: Jackie Pearce. It was designed to be light to wear and to cover an area from the sides of her nose to the back of the skull. I built strands of hair into the rear and sides of this structure to weave beneath her normal hairline. To suggest the scales I took a discarded Boa Constrictor's skin and made a female cast of this in plaster. Into this I poured plastic and upon curing it gave me a perfect snake skin material with all the marvellous patterning intact. Sections of this I fitted wherever was appropriate in the head, the cheeks, the neck and so on, until the results took on a serpent-like appearance. The extended fangs were a complete acrylic set, and fitted over all the normal front teeth from canine to canine. From another set of special fangs dripped the deadly Reptile venom – nothing to worry about – the man-killing poison was simply glycerine! This goo was released from a lozenge concealed in the roof of Jacqueline's mouth and triggered by her tongue. This appliance had been first developed by Phil Leakey whilst working on the original Dracula several years previously. The make-up for *The Reptile* took, I should say, one hour to apply from start to finish. I made the eye pieces with lenses built in. They were separate so that I could fit them just before each take so there wasn't too much discomfort for the artist while she was waiting about.

Jacqueline Pearce:

"The Reptile's face was mainly scales. The very top was painted on and then scales would be put on over the top of that. It took a long time but it was put on very early in the morning, so I was barely awake, and unlike other performers, the idea of Roy keeping me amused by singing wasn't really an option. But, I remember mostly how restricting the make-up for *The Reptile* was to work in. It was stuck on piecemeal with a kind of glue. Then at the end of the day it had to be taken off with surgical spirit. So the skin on my face was left very raw. It was not fun. It was very painful and uncomfortable, as well as being very creepy and claustrophobic. The only thing I can say is that the Reptile make-up was better than I looked when I arrived there first thing in the morning – I can tell you that! The make-up may have been wonderful, but I've always been a bit surprised over the longevity of the Hammer films I made. I know they've since become classics and people drool over them, but I've never quite understood why, because on the whole I don't think the production values were terribly good."

On this occasion, Roy was given the time and resources to more fully develop and execute his creative vision. He wasn't the only one pleased with the studio's indulgence in the appearance of the Snake Woman.

Rosemary Burrows (Wardrobe):

"We wanted something rather special for the Snake Woman to wear, which complemented Roy's fabulous design. It was Hammer's custom to rent frocks as required, or make do and mend. However, on this one occasion, they actually gave me some money to buy fabric! I found this lovely, silky fabric, which was just right. The look and feel of it was highly suggestive of the sensuality of a snake. I can't remember another time when they allowed me to go out and buy what I wanted. I was bowled over!"

Roy Ashton's design for Jackie Pearce's make-up in *The Reptile* is now considered to be among his best ever work. Even now, who could gaze on that fearsome countenance for the first time, without a shudder of repulsion. Significantly, along with his Zombie, this last of Roy's credited Hammer Monsters was a hit. He was to leave Hammer on one of the high notes of his career.

> I had been at Bray for over a decade on a picture by picture basis, doing my best to carry out the intentions of my employers. Once or twice, I received commendations from those responsible for making company policy but I received little in the way of financial encouragement. I felt as though my work was in danger of becoming stale. On the final day of shooting *The Reptile*, a producer came bouncing up towards me. 'Roy' he announced clearing his throat. 'We need you to fly to Tenerife on Sunday to replace the make-up chap on *One Million Years BC*.' 'I'm sorry. That's not possible.' I said. 'That's too short notice. You'll have to get someone else to fill in. I haven't had a break in four years and I've already arranged to take my wife on holiday!' *The Reptile* would be my last film for Hammer as Head of Make-up. I did work on a couple of other Hammer films as a special consultant. This was again without screen credit. All that would be years in the future. At that precise moment I closed up my make-up kit and said my goodbyes to my friends at Bray. I drove out of the gates of that little studio and never looked back. I had already decided to try my luck elsewhere, and whatever new challenges were to come my way.

152

A Reputation Made in Horror!

❝ As soon as I left the Hammer 'Horror Factory' as I had begun to think of it, I was quickly engaged in much larger productions. This meant a considerable amount of travel over the next two decades, across Europe, India, Africa and in the Far East. ❞

A Reputation Made in Horror!

The King of Horror.

Below:
John Carradine and friend
in The Monster Club

At the time Roy Ashton left Hammer, the studio had already produced its most highly regarded films. Roy's departure also coincided with the end of Hammer's being based at Bray Studios. The company was soon to move production to Elstree, following a deal with ABPC. The panic about financial support had already set in. American backing was diminishing, and Roy knew this would have disastrous consequences on the already chronic under-investment in make-up effects. In addition, Roy was being paid only for the days on which films were being shot. The pace was relentless, with little reward. He had never been recompensed for the weeks of design work he had been putting in between films and never relinquished his copyrights. Roy could not openly protest. As a freelance make-up designer, he would risk black-listing, and the loss of his income, as it was. The consistent use of the same personnel, which had resulted in the family atmosphere that made Hammer special, was gone. The company was now employing, as a matter of policy, new and different crews for each production. This policy most likely resulted from pressure from the American "majors", who wanted Hammer brought into line with their own production methods. The certainty of work being available to the established team had gone. The old gang started drifting away to pick up work elsewhere. Roy did not regard this time as a problem, but rather as an opportunity. He would seek to use his talents in more diversified applications, and to an extent, he succeeded. But, his reputation was made in horror, and he would forever find difficulty in abandoning the genre completely.

In Spring of 1980, Roy expressed his thoughts about Hammer's cult status, and his own difficulties in branching out, in letters written to friend and colleague, Phil Leakey:

Getting away from Horrors seems a bit difficult. Since no fantastic offers have turned up lately, I accepted an invitation from Milton Subotsky of "Sword and Sorcery Productions Limited" to do another film, shooting in April and May at EMI. I had hardly signed the letter of engagement when some other chap rang up about another "Werewolf". Oh dear!". I suppose it will always be a mystery for me that conventions are held, magazines published, and fan clubs established about those blessed films. The fans' enthusiasm remains unabated, and their

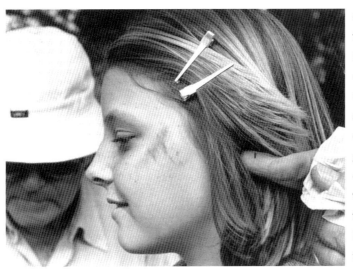

estimation of the films unaffected by my cynical views. I can't think that Carerras, Hinds and Co. had much else but financial gain in view. They don't deserve the worship of the fans. Never mind - I'm grateful for the employment

Left:
Roy studies Jodie
Foster's cheek
(Candleshoe)

Below:
Roy fits a mask for Vault

and the experience. And I don't seem to be able to get quite away from those funny old productions – *The Monster Club* – that's the title of my next – Oh dear!

Outside the Horror genre, Roy Ashton provided a wide range of make-ups for major feature films, commercials and television dramas. He created complex period make-ups for *The Private Life Of Sherlock Holmes* (1970), *Jane Eyre* (1970), *Ragtime* (1981), and *Revolution* (1983). He also worked for Walt Disney Productions on the children's fantasies: *Escape From The Dark* (1976), *Candleshoe* (1977) and *The Spaceman and King Arthur* (1979). *Candleshoe* starred Hollywood veteran, David Niven who in addition to a 'straight part' as the family retainer, wore three different character make-ups as a chauffeur, crusty old colonel and hirsute Scottish gardener. Niven appeared with an up and coming youngster: Jodie Foster.

Elizabeth Ashton:

"I went along with Roy on location, and bumped into David Niven, but Roy wouldn't introduce me. David Niven was charming but it was a very strange thing in the film industry at that time. Some of the actors treated the make-up artists and the hairdressers as servants. Roy always regarded himself as a retainer of the artists, a backing person, so he wouldn't push himself forward or be overly familiar. He regarded his work as a very formal relationship, except for Peter Cushing and Christopher Lee who were both very friendly with Roy. He did introduce me to Jodie Foster, though. Roy predicted 'She is a very clever little actress. She is going to make a name for herself.' Just look at her now!"

In the same year, Roy Ashton contributed uncredited make-up to *Star Wars* (1977). He also worked on *Flash Gordon* (1980) and *Raiders of the Lost Ark* (1981). However, few engagements gave him as much enjoyment as working with his colleague, Harry Frampton and actor Peter Sellers on the three "Pink Panther" films, which also re-united Roy with Herbert Lom.

A Reputation Made in Horror!

Due to the extremely high regard Ashton had earned as "The King of Horror", it was natural that his skills would be in demand throughout the British horror and fantasy film industry. Roy quickly established the same sort of freelance relationship with Hammer's greatest rivals Amicus Films and Tyburn Films. Amicus was headed by Milton Subotsky and Max Rosenberg, who in addition to Roy, had acquired the services of other Hammer personnel.

I don't believe there was a difference between Hammer and Amicus, from a make-up point of view. I had to pull the script to bits and find out what was required of me just the same. However, I thought the Amicus producer, Milton Subotsky, a most charming and kind person. He was a voracious reader and collected a prestigious library of volumes on all sorts of curious subjects. He was always very appreciative of what I was trying to do.

Dr. Terror's House Of Horrors (1964), starred Peter Cushing and Christopher Lee and was directed by Freddie Francis.

Freddie Francis:

"I asked for Roy on the Amicus films, because on these pictures once you start shooting you have only six weeks to do them, and you can have fun but you have got to crash on with them. I knew Roy would read the script and be fully prepared. And because I knew Roy, and the things he had done at Hammer, I knew that he would do the horror things just as well for Amicus!"

Top:
Milton Subotsky and
Roy Ashton

Above: Roy works on
Cushing's head.

Amicus revived the format of the compendium horror movie, previously used in Ealing's *Dead Of Night* (1945), and went on to produce an entire series of new British horrors. Roy contributed both monsters and special make-up effects for many of these productions. These include *The Skull* (1965), *The Deadly Bees* (1966), *Torture Garden* (1968), *The House that Dripped Blood* (1970), *Tales from the Crypt* (1971), *Asylum* (1972), *Vault of Horror* (1973), and *From Beyond the Grave* (1974).

"I don't care for today's horrible, bursting effects very much. I think the stories of Edgar Allan Poe with their mysterious atmospheres are much more acceptable. I don't like seeing people shot and killed, the parting of limbs and that sort of thing. I don't think that's necessary at all. Some of the producers seem to indulge themselves rather excessively to my way of thinking."

Rather than relying on shocking the audience, *The Skull* required the slow building of tension and disquiet. The use of Freddie Francis, who had directed Hammer's psychological thrillers, emphasised this directive style. Roy discovered that Amicus had

156

made use of more than just Hammer's personnel:

Left:
Roy adjusts an effect on Asylum

On the first day of shooting *The Skull*, I remember the prop boy was really excited about the realism of the skull we were using. Two or three people gathered to look at the grisly relic he held aloft from a canvas sack. 'What do you think of that Roy?' he asked me with pride about his find. I blushed with more than a little embarrassment when on closer inspection, he discovered my name and a date etched into the underside. I couldn't believe that it was the skull I had made for the corpse in *Paranoiac* some time before.

Another director drafted in by Amicus was Roy Ward Baker. Although Baker had directed for Hammer, like Roy he had started out in the British film industry at Gainsborough and he already had a distinguished career within the British Film Industry. Baker worked with Ashton on *Asylum* (1972), *And Now the Screaming Starts* (1973) and *Vault of Horror* (1973).

"Amicus gave me headaches, in the make-up department. Milton asked me to prepare four or five men to resemble skull-like zombies for *Vault of Horror*. It took quite a bit of effort to produce such an effect. Casting and moulding takes quite a time. So does the blending of the artist's features with the semi-mask construction, especially when you have to get them ready within an hour or so of shooting, but all was satisfactorily resolved. I like collaborating with the director, Roy Ward Baker, who is very efficient and gives precise indications. No fooling around with him!"

Above: The masks used in Vault of Horror and (Left) the masks shown in situ.

A Reputation Made in Horror!

*Roy shares a drink
with Mr. and Mrs. Roy
Ward Baker*

*The Grim
Reaper
from
Tales
from the
Crypt*

Roy Ward Baker:

"Roy was an artist. He always based his designs on nature, in many ways he was pre-eminent in the field of the grotesque and the fantastic. He was the man to have if you were going to make that type of picture. Most of the time these things kind of slot together. Kevin Francis, who produced the pictures at Tyburn, and Milton Subotsky at Amicus never really thought of using anyone else. When they were thinking of making a Horror picture the cry went out: 'Is Roy available? We must get Roy!' It became automatic!"

Although Roy was kept fully occupied by a British cinema industry which valued his abilities, on two occasions, he was asked back to Hammer to help them out with special make-ups. He was uncredited for his assistance. The first of these occasions was for *The Devil Rides Out* (1968).

I didn't do any make-up in *The Devil Rides Out*, but I made two masks for it. I think it was Tony Keys who contacted me to do them. The first one was for the Angel of Death who was supposed to come galloping in on a horse. I got a skull at home and modelled the mask as near correctly as anatomically possible, in such a way as it could be fitted over a man's face. It was a forerunner of the Grim Reaper I later created for *Tales from the Crypt*. This later apparition depended on a motorcycle rather than equine transportation. The other mask was basically goat-like, in accordance with the traditional image of the Devil.

Elizabeth Ashton:

Before the film started shooting, many things had to be prepared at home and research in museums and libraries took up much of Roy's time. Roy and I discussed the possibilities and he made some drawings, since stolen I am sorry to say."

At that time I was working on Carol Reed's production of the musical *Oliver!* at Shepperton Studios, with a colleague called George Frost . We had

to move out into the countryside on location one day and I suddenly saw a goat in a yard there. 'Good heavens, that is what I want!' I said. As soon as I had finished my commitment with George, I set to work with my sketch pad. I modelled a full sized goat's head out of plasticine again, and then cast it in plaster. Into the female mould I pressed some laminated paper, which I next overlaid with actual fleece.

Elizabeth Ashton:

"I remember him sitting in the kitchen saying 'How can I make the ears stick out and flop?' We thought about it then he said 'I know!' Then he took an old towel of mine and cut it up to make the ears. He rolled some of the towel around the cardboard centres of two toilet rolls – then hung looser towelling off the ends."

I thought that was funny, because in England we have an expression which we use when a chap doesn't take much notice or doesn't hear you: 'To have cloth ears'. Yet, I couldn't think of anything to give them rigidity. Ultimately, I took the cylinders out of two lavatory rolls and shaped the ears with them in a wonderful way, the tips of them hanging down.

Elizabeth Ashton:

"The horns were a problem, and I remember Roy sitting at the kitchen table, which was laminated plastic, modelling some out of plasticine which stuck to the table top. When he was satisfied he then made papier-mâché and laid it over the modelling clay. When this was dry, he was able to complete the horns by filling the hollows with more liquidised paper. He then wound the horns with some coarse cord."

I wound pieces of string around them right up to the top and covered them in, to match this curious spiral effect on the goat's horns. When I'd painted the final outcome it resembled the natural protuberances of the animal pretty well. The mask had to come right down over the shoulders, and that was sufficient as far as my share of the effect was concerned. They put Eddie Powell behind a sort of dais. It was the same Eddie Powell I suggested years ago, when I worked on *The Mummy*, as a double for Chris Lee, since he had the most fantastic likeness to him.

Christopher Lee:

"Dennis Wheatley was very happy with *The Devil Rides Out*. But think what you could do with that film now? I could do it again today, if somebody would let me have the money. The Angel of Death and all the other manifestations could be absolutely electrifying. The Goat of Mendies: 'The Devil himself' – poor Eddie Powell did that. They covered him up with this horrible thing sitting there in the dark in Black Park. So many films of Hammer were made there. It was very effective."

Eddie Powell:

"It was a bit chilly. I was standing in a hole on top of a rock made out of plaster. I was covered with large bits of skin. Nobody had to worry about the Devil's legs as you never saw them. I had some extremely hairy artificial legs sticking out in front of me. These were jointed so it looked as though I was sitting crossed legged."

Hands of the Ripper is an extremely gruesome reworking of Jack The Ripper story and was Roy Ashton's final Hammer film. The make-up was supervised by Bunty Phillips, but it was Roy who was called upon to fashion one spectacular effect. Arousing the psychopathic rage of "The Ripper", prostitute Long Liz (Lynda Baron) has a hat pin pushed through her eye.

I made an almost complete eye with lids, eyelashes and everything. I made it out of perspex, with an iris painted on the back. In the centre I drilled a hole with a shaft protruding, representing the hat pin. I applied all this underneath Lynda Baron's brow. Now, I had agreed to do this on the condition that I could conduct her down to the studio floor, stand by while she was being photographed, and guide her back upstairs to take the whole contraption off again. It was indeed a dangerous enterprise: she had to walk with that object sticking out there and if you have one eye shut you can't see too well...

Hands Of The Ripper was denounced by critics as the most violent Hammer film ever made. In previous years this accusation would have been exploited in order to attract cinema audiences. However, in the USA, Universal insisted on the scene being censored to ease distribution.

The final effect didn't come out as effectively as I had hoped: it was just a flash. They should have shown the job more in detail, especially as it had been a long complicated one. So it was a lot of labour which was mostly wasted, to my way of thinking.

Roy Ashton had one further encounter with the character that brought him into horror make-up back in 1956. *Frankenstein – The True Story* (1973), was originally made for television by Universal as a three-hour special.

That was a lengthy film, I was there for six months! Harry Frampton made up Michael Sarrazin as the Monster, while I took care of all the others: James Mason, David McCallum, Leonard Whiting, and Sir Ralph Richardson. We might well hold the record for the number of damaged limbs, diseased faces and general oddities made for any one production. You will recollect we also had a crawling arm in the picture, which was actually cast from mine again. Within the latex special effects constructed a radio controlled mechanism, operated out of sight by a fellow named Roy Whybrow, who had five or six technicians seconding him. That was really a most eerie sort of effect, turning out much more convincing than the hand we previously used in *Dr. Terror's House of Horrors.*

Kevin Francis, the son of Freddie Francis, created yet another successful British horror film company, Tyburn Films. Freddie directed some of Tyburn's more successful outings, including *The Ghoul* (1974), from an original screenplay by Tony Hinds (operating under his nom-de-plume of John Elder).

People often think that such an assignment is most complicated, though it is much easier to create a very old and horrible looking character than a very nice and neat new one!

"Dracula's loveliest victim", Veronica Carlson was a featured player in *The Ghoul*.

Veronica Carlson:

"Roy Ashton made me look beautiful. He made me see myself so differently, Roy knew what was best for me. He would let me do my own eyebrows. He would let me find my own arch, but he was the only one who could follow the arch as I liked it. It was an education to sit in a chair with a man like that and say: 'Go ahead and just do it' and know that it was going to be wonderful. The final touch was the cheek bones because I was always accused of having a full face. It was even suggested at one time that I should have teeth extracted to get the hollow cheekbones effect. But I couldn't wait for Roy to apply the blusher that was the crowning touch. I used to look forward to that more than anything."

Tales From The Crypt (1972), is regarded by many as Roy Ashton's post-Hammer masterpiece. The film featured an all-star cast, including Sir Ralph Richardson. He may have chosen to appear in a horror film, but Sir Ralph refused to cackle or wear a ghoulish character make-up as the famous Cryptkeeper. "The producers wanted the Cryptkeeper to be made up complete with beard and everything. I told them that my face is quite old enough and does not need to be disguised one bit to make me appear ancient." quipped Sir Ralph. Reunited with Peter Cushing in a story called *Poetic Justice*, Roy Ashton designed and produced what director Freddie Francis described as "the most horrific make-up that Peter Cushing ever had to wear."

The role of Grimsdyke was a personal triumph for both artists. When Peter Cushing turned down the role of Maitland in another story, Milton Subotsky asked him if he would like the part of Arthur Grimsdyke. Cushing immediately sought to personalise the role. The old man, Grimsdyke, was supposed to be silent throughout the story, but Peter felt that dialogue was crucial. Also, Peter incorporated numerous references to his recently deceased wife, Helen. "To millions who watch this type of picture, the horror must be utterly believable otherwise the whole effect fails." Cushing declared. In the film, Grimsdyke is a kind-hearted pensioner whose property becomes a safe haven for abandoned pets and the local children. "I based the character of Grimsdyke on an old man I once knew. He was rich, but wore shabby clothes all the time, and he was good to the kids in the neighbourhood." However the pensioner's reputation is destroyed through a relentless hate campaign by neighbour James Elliott (Robin Phillips). Separated from his animal companions and branded a child abuser, Grimsdyke is shunned by the local community. His heart broken, the old man takes his own life. "But it isn't all goody-goody for me", Cushing stated once in an interview. "I do manage to come back from the grave and wreak ghostly revenge on the evildoer".

"In his grave after it had been filled in, Mr. Grimsdyke slept... and little by little, as the days passed, the juices in his body began to ferment. The juices bubbled silently and then gave way to a host of maggots, and the flesh of Mr Grimsdyke's face rotted away a bit at a time, until what was left of his cheeks and his mouth clung only in patches to the bare skull beneath. His fingers became claws on which oddly the fingernails continued to grow, and his arms became mere sticks of bone under disintegrating cloth."

Jack Oleck, Tales From The Crypt (1972)

Peter Cushing from *Past Forgetting* (1988)

"Roy Ashton a dear man of gentle disposition and an expert make-up artist, took care of that department when I played Mr. Grimsdyke in *Tales from the Crypt*. The moment when that character emerged from his grave, having spent quite a spell underground, was scheduled for shooting immediately after lunch, up to which time I had to look normal. Roy kindly gave up his hour break in order to get me ready for resurrection. I possessed an ugly set of false teeth, acquired from the BBC when I was playing Sherlock Holmes (that man of many disguises) in *The Greek Interpreter*. Roy agreed that these would fit the bill perfectly, helping to give me a skull-like visage, but the empty eye sockets presented a bit of a problem. I asked Roy if he could use black gauze which I would be able to see through, instead of Max Factor painted over my eyelids, because that might have made me look like a panda. He could and he did. After matting my hair with real mud, and colouring my face lustreless grey, the effect we were after was achieved in about forty five minutes, giving us time to snatch a sandwich and a glass of milk before we were called on the set."

Peter Cushing as Grimsdyke

The make-up was applied to Peter Cushing's face with pieces I had previously prepared from laminated paper to suggest severe wasting of features. To accentuate the skull-like appearance I fabricated shapes and built them up around each eye. Within those, I simply fastened a piece of an old

black costume my wife used to have, since matt black doesn't photograph and he should appear to be sightless. Peter could still look through the nylon, but we couldn't see his eyes beneath the fabric. I brought the hair forward and made it very lank and filthy-looking. This is an operation you can do in a few seconds with grease paint, dirt and various bits of rubbish. A slight growth of beard combined with prominent teeth to complete the effect. By the way, do you know about that curious incident with the spider on the headstone? Well, everything was arranged and Peter was put into the grave, covered up with rushes and grass. Just as they turned the camera over, I noticed a spider in the upper corner of the gravestone. How it got there, heaven only knows... As the action started, the spider descended as Peter ascended and waited quite close to Grimsdyke's face. I thought that was very good. Now, for safety's sake, Freddie decided to have an extra take and bless me if the spider conveniently returned to its starting position on take number two ready to start its action all over again!"

Roy and Peter Cushing's plaster head

For his performance in *Tales From The Crypt*, Peter Cushing received the Licorne d'Or Award for the Best Actor of 1973.

> **I think that horror and fantasy can still mystify, interest, and puzzle the audience, without being repugnant. I am convinced we will go back to a more romantic, more colourful cinema. After all, one of the greatest gifts which God has granted to man is the faculty of imagination, since it is a creative thing: you use that in order to make pictures within yourself, to build a wonderful world. If we learn to use that power and to transport ourselves into what could be heaven while still on earth, then the future holds much for us all.**

Epilogue

By Bob Keen (Master Monster Maker)

When I was a small child I would sneak into our living room in the middle of the night and turn the television on, turning the volume down so I wouldn't wake the rest of the house and I would wait for one of the late night Hammer films to come on. Whilst these films would scare the pants off me, I was fascinated by the people who could make these nightmares breathe. I would wait until the end of the film not wanting to end this secret pleasure, I would watch every credit to the end wondering what the various people who made these films did with their bewildering names and titles. After a while, I started to realise that two names would constantly reappear under the less-than-interesting title of "Make-up by.." - the two masters that I refer to were Phil Leakey and Roy Ashton.

By watching these credits go by, it dawned on my young brain that these must be the people who create the monsters and I became fascinated on trying to find anything in print about their work. You have to realise at that time there were very limited resources to give the information on these backroom wizards. It was Roy Ashton's werewolf make-up on Oliver Reed that inspired me to persuade my parents to buy me the various make-up materials to create my own monsters. With this, myself and my patient friends soon discovered that what Roy had achieved on the screen was very difficult to reproduce. Some thirty years later, I now find myself in the envious position of running a full-time make-up effects lab in Pinewood Studios.

Even though today's effects are for a more sophisticated audience, I look back in wonder at how people like Roy and Phil achieved such great effects with such limited resources. To say that they were pioneers underestimates their true skills. I have nothing but admiration for them and thank them for inspiring me to follow a career in make-up effects. Without Roy Ashton or Phil Leakey, I do not think that the British make-up effects industry would ever have grown and blossomed into what it is today.

Roy Ashton
Make-upography

The following is an almost complete list of films on which Roy Ashton was
chief make-up artist, or assistant.

Tudor Rose (1936)
The Man Who Changed his Mind (1936)
Jack of All Trades (1936)
Windbag The Sailor (1936)
Good Morning Boys (1937)
Oh Mister Porter! (1937)
Dr. Syn (1937)
Old Bones Of The River (1938)
The Rope (1938),
The Challenge (1938)
Ask A Policeman (1938)
Prison Without Bars (1938)
Captain Horatio Hornblower RN (1951)
Moulin Rouge (1952).
Mr Arkadin (1954)
Invitation To The Dance (1954)
Bhowani Junction (1954)
Fire Maidens from Outer Space (1956)
Pickup Alley (1957)
The Curse of Frankenstein (1957)
The Whole Truth (1958)
Dunkirk (1958)
Sea Of Sand (1958)
Dracula (1958)
The Revenge Of Frankenstein (1958)
Circus Of Horrors (1959)
The Hound Of The Baskerville (1959)
The Ugly Duckling(1959)
Yesterday's Enemy(1959)
The Mummy(1959)
The Man Who Could Cheat Death(1959)
The Stranglers of Bombay(1960)
The Curse Of The Werewolf(1960)
The Brides Of Dracula(1960)
Never Take Sweets From A Stranger(1960)
The Two Faces Of Dr Jekyll (1960)
The Shadow of the Cat (1961)
Gorgo (1961)
Visa To Canton(1961)
Watch It Sailor!(1961)
The Terror Of The Tongs(1961)
The Phantom Of The Opera(1962)
Captain Clegg (1962)
The Pirates of Blood River(1962)
Maniac (1963)
The Damned(1963)
The Crimson Blade(1963)
Cash on Demand(1963)
Paranoiac (1963)
Kiss Of The Vampire (1964)
The Evil Of Frankenstein (1964)

Nightmare (1964)
The Devil Ship Pirates (1964)
The Gorgon (1964)
The Curse Of The Mummy's Tomb (1964)
Guns at Batasi (1964)
The Pink Panther (1964)
Dr. Terror's House of Horrors (1964)
The Skull (1965)
Die! Die! My Darling! (1965)
Fanatic (1965)
She (1965)
The Secret of Blood Island (1965)
Hysteria (1965)
The Brigand of Kandahar (1965)
The Deadly Bees (1966)
Dracula Prince Of Darkness (1966)
The Plague Of The Zombies (1966)
Rasputin The Mad Monk (1966)
The Reptile (1966)
The Old Dark House (1966)
Oliver! (1968)
Torture Garden (1968)
The Devil Rides Out (1968)
2001: A Space Odyssey (1968)
The Jokers (1968)
The Private Life Of Sherlock Holmes (1970)
Jane Eyre (1970)
The House that Dripped Blood (1970)
Hands Of The Ripper (1971)
Kidnapped (1971)
The Devils (1971)
Tales From The Crypt (1972)
The Creeping Flesh (1972)
Asylum (1972)
Vault of Horror (1973)
Frankenstein – The True Story (1973)
The Ghoul (1974)
Persecution (1974)
The Beast Must Die (1974)
Return of the Pink Panther (1974)
The Hit (1974)
Escape From The Dark (1976)
Pink Panther Strikes Again (1976)
Candleshoe (1977)
Star Wars (1977)
The Spaceman And King Arthur (1979)
Flash Gordon (1980)
Little Lord Fauntleroy (1980)
The Monster Club (1980)
Raiders of the Lost Ark (1981)
Revolution (1983)
The Masks Of Death (1984)
War & Remembrance (1988)